SILE

SILENCED SCREAMS

Surviving Anesthetic Awareness
During Surgery: A True-life Account

Jeanette M. Liska

AANA PUBLISHING, INC.
COUNCIL FOR PUBLIC INTEREST IN ANESTHESIA
PARK RIDGE, ILLINOIS

AANA Publishing, Inc.
222 South Prospect Avenue
Park Ridge, IL 60068-4001

Printed in the United States of America

Last digit indicates print number: 10 9 8 7 6 5 4 3 2 1

The author(s) and publisher have done everything possible to make this book accurate, up to date, and in accord with accepted standards at the time of publication. The authors, editors, and publisher are not responsible for errors or omissions or for consequences from application of the book, and make no warranty, expressed or implied, in regard to the contents of the book. Any practice described in this book should be applied by the reader in accordance with professional standards of care used in regard to the unique circumstances that may apply in each situation.

Library of Congress Cataloging-in-Publication Data
Liska, Jeanette M.
    Silenced screams / Jeanette M. Liska.
        p. ; cm.
    Includes bibliographical references.
    ISBN 0-9700279-3-1 (pbk. : alk. paper)
    1. Liska, Jeanette M.--Health. 2. Anesthesia--Complications--Biography.
3. Awareness. 4. Surgical errors. 5. Pain. [DNLM: 1. Anesthesia--adverse effects--Personal Narratives. 2. Awareness. 3. Medical Errors. 4. Monitoring, Intraoperative. WO 245 L769s 2002] I. AANA Publishing, Inc. Council for Public Interest in Anesthesia. II. Title.

RD82.5 .L55 2002
617.9'6041'092--dc21   2002014160

Cover photo © Creatas/Picturequest

TABLE OF CONTENTS

ACKNOWLEDGMENTS vii

PROLOGUE 1

CHAPTER 1   **My Own Story**..11
          "A short rest..."

CHAPTER 2   **A Problem Without a Name**.........................27
          "...the invisible scars of surgery."

CHAPTER 3   **A Living Testimony**...................................39
          "...nothing could possibly go wrong."

CHAPTER 4   **Aftermath** 51
          "...nowhere to turn for compassion or solace."

CHAPTER 5   **Looking Out the Window**.............................61
          "I flash back with every breath I take."

CHAPTER 6   **Symposium**...85
          "A miracle...to go."

CHAPTER 7   **AWARE is Born** 91
          "Awareness With Anesthesia Research Education"

CHAPTER 8   **Passage to Freedom** 105
          "What we don't know can hurt us."

CHAPTER 9   **Mainstream Media Exposure Reveals the Truth** 115
          "....willingness to speak out."

CHAPTER 10   **Healing** 139
          "You have the answers within you."

CHAPTER 11   **Anesthesia in the 21st Century** 147
A Journey of Progress
by Sandra M. Ouellette, CRNA, MEd, FAAN and
Richard G. Ouellette, CRNA, MEd

CHAPTER 12   **Intraoperative Awareness**..173
A Clinical Discussion for Providers and Patients
by Sandra M. Ouellette, CRNA, MEd, FAAN and
Richard G. Ouellette, CRNA, MEd

APPENDIX   **Awareness in the Media** 191

irst and foremost, I would like to thank God for the experience. It was within those minutes, hours, days and years that I grew into new awareness of self, understanding, forgiveness and change. Thanks be to you, Lord. I am forever grateful.

A special thank you to my wonderful daughters Lisa and Valerie. I am proud of you in so many ways, but most of all for your strength. Thank you for being there throughout these years. Thank you for believing in me and for your endless love and support. Thank you for being my angels. My prayer is that I have been able to teach you faith, hope and love, to always follow your dreams, to help others, and to live your passion to its fullest. I love you with all my heart and I thank you with all my soul. Life sometimes is not about you, but what you do in it.

Another special thank you to my husband David, son Brian and grandson Dominic. I love you so much for bringing joy to my life. Thank you for all your help and understanding through the many long hours and days when I was working to finish this book. Thank you for all your "I Love Yous" and believing in me and what I was trying to do to help others cope with the aftermath of awareness during anesthesia. David, you are a wonderful husband, father, doctor, and you are my best friend. Brian, live your dreams and trust God to guide you. My sweet grandson Dominic, Nana hopes one day you'll look back at all this hard work Nana did and smile with pride. I love you all so very much. Thank you for everything.

I thank my family for their love and support. Thanks to my mom, sister Diane, and brother Bill—I love you.

Thank you to Dr. and Mrs. Liska, Terri, Dennis, Linda, Julie, Mary and Jerry Anderson.

I would now like to thank those in anesthesia who have stood by my side. You are also my angels. With love and respect I would like to thank the following people for helping me heal, continue my work, and bring this book with honor to all those who read it: Christopher Bettin, Rita Rupp, Suzanne Brown, Richard and Sandra Ouellette, Craig Atkins, Bette Wildgust, Maureen Witte, Theresa Kole, Peter Ogren. Thank you also to all who have invited me to speak on awareness during anesthesia and supported my work, including Dr. Peter Sebel, Dr. Hank Bennett, Dr. Charles Moleskey, Dr. Anthony Messina, Dr. Janet Osteman, and Dr. Andrew Kojka. To all the pharmaceutical companies that have sponsored my lectures, thank you. A special thank you to the media for helping me reach thousands of others who have experienced awareness, as well as their families and friends. Thank you Oprah, Bill Ritter with *20/20*, Leeza, Tom Snyder, *Dateline, Inside Edition, Extra*, CNN, ABC, CBS, NBC, *Fox News, TLC, Redbook, Time Magazine, U.S. News & World Report, Newsweek, People, Allure, First for Women* and all the others. Thank you for your help and most of all your kindness and understanding for what I went through with my own anesthesia awareness. God bless you and keep you safe as you do your work.

Thank you to my friends Col. Raymond and Dianne Cole, Linda Ferris, Francis and Maja Simone, Jennie Linsey, Sgt. Major Charles L. and Dahrie Hayman, General and Mrs. Charles Wilhelm, General and Mrs. Francis Libutti, General and Mrs. Anthony Zinni, Ed and Missy Horn, Tom Perez, Stephen Hungerford, Lt. Eddie Reyes, General and Mrs. John Grinolds, Don and Karen Hellwig, Bob and Linda Malm, Joe and Nancy Kovalik, Kelly and John Zaunn, Jeannetta Yzzuf, Richard Muscarella, Bob and Donna Tkachyk, Dr. Ted Quigley, and Danny Pietryk. Thank you also to Dr. Michael A. Lobatz, Dr. Christine A. Baser, and Dr. Howard Richmond.

FOREWORD

his book comes to all those who have experienced awareness during anesthesia, with passion from my heart and soul. I hope this book brings understanding, help and hope to your healing. You may not be able to forget, but you can heal in time and become stronger and wiser than you ever thought you were. You are all part of God's plan to bring about positive change in anesthesia. Know you are never alone and always loved. Many blessings and thank you all for your help.

Love,

Dr. Jeanette Liska

ABOUT THE AUTHORS

Jeanette M. Liska, PhD, is dedicated to patient and healthcare provider education in the area of anesthesia awareness, with an emphasis on therapy and research. She holds a doctorate in divinity and a doctorate in pastoral psychology, and is the founder and president of AWARE (Awareness With Anesthesia Research Education). Jeanette has been interviewed about her story for numerous publications and television programs (see appendix).

Contributors: Sandra M. Ouellette has been a Certified Registered Nurse Anesthetist (CRNA) for 33 years. She is director of the Anesthesia Program at Wake Forest University Baptist Medical Center/The University of North Carolina at Greensboro in Winston-Salem, North Carolina. Richard G. Ouellette, a CRNA for 33 years, is a staff anesthetist at Moses Cone Health System/Wesley Long Campus in Greensboro, North Carolina. The Ouellettes are well-known speakers on the topic of anesthetic awareness.

ABOUT THE COUNCIL FOR PUBLIC INTEREST IN ANESTHESIA OF THE AMERICAN ASSOCIATION OF NURSE ANESTHETISTS

Founded by the American Association of Nurse Anesthetists (AANA), the Council for Public Interest in Anesthesia has monitored issues that affect the public interest in matters of nurse anesthesia practice since 1988.

The AANA itself was founded in 1931 and is located in Park Ridge, Illinois. It is the professional organization for more than 28,000 Certified Registered Nurse Anesthetists (CRNAs). As advanced practice nurses, CRNAs administer approximately 65 percent of the 26 million anesthetics delivered in the United States each year. CRNAs practice in every setting where anesthesia is available and are the sole anesthesia providers in more than two-thirds of all rural hospitals.

For additional information on the AANA or the council, call 847-692-7050, or go to www.aana.com or www.AnesthesiaPatientSafety.com.

odern medicine. An ocean of comfort and confidence rests quietly within the bounds of those five simple syllables. Although we revile the garbage spewing from the boob-tube, kick our automobiles for their planned obsolescence and paper-thin chassis, and curse the buzzing and blinking host of computerized contraptions complicating our already too-harried lives, one aspect of modernity is rarely questioned, let alone despised. Standing pristine and solemn amidst visions of sanitized research laboratories and shining instruments, modern medicine is an island of virtue floating in the swamp of sleek decadence that has come to typify our modern world. Exalted far above the bustling mediocrity that has become the norm in recent years, modern medicine holds a uniquely privileged position. In a society where cynicism runs rampant, this single discipline still inspires pride, if not actual reverence.

There are good reasons for the special place modern medicine holds in our hearts—not airy, theoretical ones, but rock-hard, purely practical ones. Ask anyone who's been pulled from the gasping brink of a heart attack, or healed of an otherwise fatal infection, or had sight restored after slipping behind cataracts' ever-darkening veils. We've all heard tales of miraculous healings, perhaps we've even experienced them personally.

"Miracle" is appropriate to describe what has become commonplace in medicine. For although we may take our flush toilets and telephones and electric lights for granted, there is something just a little godlike about what medical practice has become in a few short decades. The very secrets of life, from the molecules that enable us to think to the genes that shape our frames, are read like a book by today's scientist-physicians who have stepped into the shoes of the so-called "healers" of old. Even the most hardened can only shake their heads in wonder at how far medicine has come in such a short time.

Think back to the state of medical practice just 150 years ago. Doctoring was an uncertain and sometimes foul business then, an arena ruled more by guesswork than by knowledge, and rightly considered to have more in common with the mystical arts than the sciences. In those days, even for the well-to-do, hospitals were often looked upon as places to meet a horrible fate instead of as healing palaces. So awful was the prospect of surgery that it was quite common for the afflicted to mutilate themselves or simply go without treatment of any kind rather than submit to the torment of the physician's knife.

It was the sorry state of surgery, in particular, which gave hospitals their unsavory reputation. With sanitation virtually nonexistent, infections often ran rampant through the wards, decimating those fortunate enough to have survived the barbaric procedures themselves. The old European operating rooms bore striking resemblances to butcher shops, a parallel that was not lost on even the dullest wits of the period.

What actually went on behind those hospital walls, however, made the quick savagery of slaughterhouses pale by comparison. Perhaps only the callused likes of medieval inquisitors, inured to the implements and horrors of the torture chamber, could feel at home in such grim halls.

Imagine what it must have been like for a patient facing even a minor operation. As you are bound tightly to a filthy table with thick leather straps, you tremble at inhuman bellows and screams reverberating through every wall from rooms beyond. A bit of warm brandy, instead of calming, rouses you temporarily to full awareness of what is to follow. Fully comprehending your urge to turn back at this point, the attending physicians no longer listen to your pleas for "just a little more time." The doctors know full well there's nothing to gain from delay except more anxiety. And there's quite enough of that already; the air literally stinks with terror. So they busy themselves with the preparations, pretending you've said nothing.

Gritting your teeth, you confront your surgeon, who has steeled himself for the occasion by relying on the same bottle of musky liquid courage from which you previously imbibed. Gazing at you sadly for a moment, he nods a secret signal to someone near the door then turns away. Taking their cue, a pair of grim-faced attendants, burly enough to hold you down should you writhe free of your restraints, wheel you through a short corridor. Other patients groan miserably as you pass by but some are far beyond that. They merely lie pale and still on the gurneys where they died of shock or infection, their mindless gazes seeping out into eternity's distance. A cold sweat oozes from your pores as your own eyes, now wide with terror, barely manage to focus upon the blood-splattered walls of the operating room. Faces, mask-like and impassive, dodge back and forth. Although you want to speak, to say something to mitigate the hideous indignity which threatens, your mouth is dry as sand. What is there to say? Only fear exists. And there's no time offered to think, for the cutting begins immediately.

The surgeon wielding the scalpel could not afford to waste precious time or energy on empathy. Operations meant pain—there was no other way. In those days, the skill of a surgeon was not determined by his anatomical knowledge or even the degree of his manual dexterity. What counted most was speed, pure and simple. Like war, the humanity of the act lay only

3

in its brevity. Some noted surgeons could amputate a leg in 30 seconds. The less adept paid a price that imperiled more than their reputations. For the physical and emotional trauma experienced by patients was so immense that it inevitably took a significant toll on both sides of the knife. The unrelenting, pathetic screams of hapless surgical patients were jackhammers, slowly but surely shattering the sanity of surgeon and patient alike. While no patient could undergo more than a few operations in a lifetime, doctors witnessed surgery routinely. The psychological toll was considerable.

Today, at the dawn of a new millennium, we find ourselves looking back at that bygone era of medical torment with a mixture of horror and amusement. We shake our heads at the thought that our not-so-distant forebears viewed surgical intervention as a frightful trial to be avoided at any cost rather than a beneficial interlude. And we cannot help but experience a sinking feeling at the notion that only a slight accident of birth separates now from then, us from them, making *our* most difficult medical experiences relatively benign while *theirs* were nothing less than hellish in the most literal sense of the word.

It is hard to believe that European and American men and women took such trials in stride as a matter of course. Contemplating what once was, we breathe a grateful sigh of relief. Modern medicine stands tall because it has come so far in the blink of a historical eye; none are so insensitive or ignorant that they are completely unaware of the distance traversed.

But where exactly was the line drawn between old and new medicine? Where did one stop and the other start? Experts can and do point to a variety of societal factors, all of which skirt the issue rather than addressing it head on. It is true that the healing arts gradually took on a distinctly rational aura during the 19th century, consistent with the dawning realization among men of science that not only the inanimate cosmos but also animate nature were subject to mathematical law. Depending more on the results of repeatable experimentation than the vagaries of anecdote, and discarding the old mantle of intuitive insight, medicine gained triumph after triumph by regarding the

4

human body as no more than an incredibly complex machine. In addition, a host of new discoveries augmented medicine's original paltry arsenal: developments in pharmacology, microbiology, and diagnostics, to name but a few, opened broad new vistas of understanding for biologists and physicians alike.

However, it is vital to recognize that not all of the technological marvels that led us out of those bad old days were of equal significance to the status medicine would eventually enjoy. A few developments were much more compelling than others. Some of the most awe-inspiring were often spelled out in strange-sounding terms beginning with "a," "an," or "anti"—all Greek prefixes implying negation. Thus, antibiotics negate germs within us, while antiseptics negate germs outside. Antitoxins neutralize biological poisons, while antipyretics quench the fires of raging fevers. Like a phalanx of Greek heroes, the negators crushed ranks of mankind's ancient scourges, gaining vigor with every new victory. More than any other factors, technocratic or sociological, these potent negators transformed and remade medicine into the tower of strength that we now recognize and cherish.

It is significant to note that the most powerful negator of the lot gained its ground over the most subtle object of all: our very awareness. To this day, it is this remarkable, undisputed chief of the negators which, more than any other single factor, carries the keys to modern medicine's kingdom: anesthesia. For it is anesthesia that negates consciousness, obliterating pain in the process. Anesthesia came to biology like an angel, a saving grace, changing the face of medicine forever. With anesthesia, the agony that tore operating theaters apart ended, and calm, systematic surgery—surgery as we now know it—began in earnest. The reassuringly quiet, clean operating rooms we take for granted and identify with modern medicine at its most efficient are, above all, the product of anesthesia. In addition, anesthesia gave doctors the breathing room they needed to study living bodies and refine surgical techniques. By allowing deliberation to replace speed, it placed the human body in the penetrating light of intellect as never before. While patients slept, physicians could think.

Modern medicine without anesthesia would be absolutely inconceivable. With anesthesia we move in a single sure leap from the torture chamber's madness to the laboratory's infinite care. Cutting into the human body has never been a step taken lightly nor by the faint of heart. However, given the agony which used to be part and parcel of such procedures, perhaps the stoutest hearts of all belonged to those who voluntarily assented to go "under the knife." We vent a justifiable sigh of relief when we contrast the blissful unconsciousness of modern surgery with the operating room nightmares of old. It is hard even to conceive the torment which used to be involved when the fragile human casing was laid open. Like a child waking up from a terrible dream, we no longer find any cause for fear. Has any facet of our history been more happily left behind and forgotten?

Single-handedly, anesthesia has wrought these immense changes. When we contemplate surgery, we are justifiably complacent; we are confident that the leering demon of unbearable pain has, once and for all, been banished into sleep's tightly stoppered flask. Or *has* it? How can we entertain doubts about something so obvious? Dare we ask such a question in the light of anesthesia's unequivocal success? This book's premise is not only that we should but that we must. For the science of anesthesiology contains some definite gaps in technology and knowledge that have not been systematically addressed until very recently.

Because anesthesia is so familiar, we tend to forget that it is a comparatively new technology. Its novelty is all the more apparent when we consider that it deals not so much with the staid laws of physics and chemistry as with the living, mercurial mind—that which makes us human.

The birth of anesthesia was not welcome; it was, on the contrary, painful and difficult. Anesthesia frightened princes, theologians, and philosophers alike, because it signaled not only an enormously burgeoning respect for science but also science's newly claimed right to infringe on what had traditionally been sacred territory: human consciousness. The very notion that chemical agents could be tailored to turn human awareness on and off like a switch involved enormous changes in Western society's basic concepts of self, free will, and the role of the divine.[1(pp16-17)]

Although painkilling drugs which leave consciousness largely unimpaired—analgesics—were known in Europe for centuries, their use was looked upon with feelings ranging from distaste to outright condemnation. In 1591, for example, Eufame Macalyane, a wealthy Scottish woman, was burned at the stake for seeking relief from pain during childbirth. British sailors requiring amputations after battles could turn to nothing more for solace than a bit of rum. When, in 1799, Sir Humphry Davy discovered that inhaled nitrous oxide could produce temporary and reversible general anesthesia, his findings were universally ignored by the medical establishment.[1(pp3-4)] The very concept of general anesthesia was simply too radical. For physicians and clergy of the day, anesthesia stepped directly over the line of propriety into taboo territory. It did not simply reduce the perception of pain; by dimming or obliterating normal consciousness, anesthesia entirely wiped out any perception of painful stimuli. Hadn't Holy Writ stipulated that women must bear children in pain? Wasn't pain the justly ordained fruit for man's sinfulness and rebellion since the time of Genesis? To interfere too much with pain was akin to blasphemy—it smacked of playing God.

Throughout the first half of the 19th century, a tiny handful of progressive physicians and dentists braved condemnation and pushed for anesthesia's acceptance into medical practice. Many more, such as Crawford Long, a prominent American surgeon, employed it secretly.[1(pp5-6)] Not surprisingly, prudence and silence usually won the day over scientific truth. When William Morton demonstrated in 1846 how a tumor could be removed under anesthesia without causing discomfort, doctors greeted the news with resounding silence.[1(pp11-12)] At last, in 1853, the tide turned with decisive suddenness. Queen Victoria accepted chloroform when giving birth to Prince Leopold, her eighth child, thus launching a new era on its way with appropriately royal benediction.[1(pp16-17)]

Yet, a little over a century of surgical anesthesia has not fully put to rest the problem of precisely what happens when consciousness is artificially darkened by chemical means. While the issue may seem more philosophical than practical at this point in time, it is anything but. Despite our apparent pinpoint control of awareness, the mechanics of this process remain as elusive as the quality of human nature itself. And because what it means to be awake and aware cannot be defined with precision, their polar opposites, unconsciousness and unawareness, also cannot be firmly tied down.

Which brings us to the subject matter of this book. Most people believe that anesthesia has forever brought an end to surgical agony, that the days when operations were performed on fully conscious patients have been left far behind in the era of buggy whips and gaslight. We trust that even major surgery will involve nothing more inconvenient than a few days off from work and a bit of soreness afterwards. Most of all, we feel confident that for every moment the scalpel flashes and innards are laid bare, we will feel nothing, perceive nothing, sense nothing.

We trust that an operation means only a short sleep, but sleep which, for its entire duration, is profound and total. As we have seen, a significant measure of our contentment with modern medicine rests squarely on this foundation of complete confidence in anesthesia. Knowing that we will not suffer unbridled pain allows us to undergo the most serious operations with relative confidence and assurance.

Doctors and patients have learned to count on this confidence. It is a critical element in the prestige that modern medical practitioners enjoy. But how well founded is this trust? Does anesthesia always work in the fashion we believe it will? Unfortunately, the answer is no. One of the most closely guarded secrets of our "painless" operating rooms is that anesthesia, the very soul of 20th century surgery, has remained an art as well as a science. And like all arts, there are occasions when it falls far short of its calculated

8

ends. When this occurs, the results can be catastrophic. Severe pain is awful enough, but nothing in the world is as terrible as a breach of heartfelt trust. When the two coincide, there is tragedy.

Until recently, the failures of general anesthesia were rarely discussed professionally among surgeons and anesthesia providers. Too much was at stake. Healthcare providers, like all of us, are not eager to jeopardize hard-earned gains, whether professional or individual. But social factors, too, work unconsciously yet subtly to enforce silence. Human nature has not changed since the days when Scripture overruled science. Although the latter is ascendant, blasphemy still exists. Only now, it is technology rather than divine right which cannot be questioned.

The anesthesia we count on everyday did not become reality overnight. The subject of endless political, theological, and social wrestling matches, it gained acceptance only after a protracted and difficult struggle which left many marks on the way the entire medical profession is viewed. In truth, these fights were so bitter and so heated that today anesthesia cannot be separated from the powerful profession that utilizes it. Anesthesia has become a vested interest.

This book deals with what happens when anesthesia fails. It is a frightening and controversial subject, made all the more difficult because it seriously calls into question things we have been taught to believe about modern medicine, its respected practitioners, and especially its scientific base. Specifically, it deals with those cases where awareness has overpowered anesthesia, resurrecting a host of horrors usually relegated to the past. It is a story, too, of cowardice and courage, of venality and altruism, for when anesthesia fails, the light of awareness illuminates us all.

REFERENCE

1. Thatcher VS. *History of Anesthesia With Emphasis on the Nurse Specialist.* Philadelphia, Pa: JB Lippincott; 1953.

CHAPTER 1

MY OWN STORY
"A short rest..."

or the briefest instant I thought I must have been dreaming. There was no possible way I could hear the doctor and nurse conversing in the operating room, yet that was precisely what was happening.

"Here's one in pretty good shape," the nurse chuckled.

The physician anesthesiologist grunted affirmatively. "Yeah, not bad at all. And she's had two kids."

My abdomen felt cold, exposed. Then I noticed that a coarse, circular piece of cloth was being laid over it. I thought, "What on earth is this? Why can't I open my eyes?"

The nurse spoke again. Her voice sounded as if her mouth was almost pressed to my ear. "What does she do, anyway?"

"Model." The anesthesiologist's voice was laden with sarcasm. "She's a TV producer, too."

The nurse laughed. Clearly, they were talking about me. I wanted to sit up and tell them to go to hell, but I couldn't move a muscle. Even my eyes were shut tightly, as if they had been sewn up. *What was going on?*

Most people don't realize there are over 150 different ways of compounding general anesthetic.

My brain snapped into an incredible state of alertness as I struggled to find an acceptable answer. There was none. Only a few minutes earlier, this very same doctor had been talking to me in soothing tones as he prepared me for a routine hernia repair. It was October 1990, at a hospital in Texas.

I recalled how, at the time, I had appreciated his reassurances. I had certainly experienced a trying few days leading up to the surgery. While dining in a restaurant, I had bitten into a shard of glass that had found its way into the beef stroganoff. My tongue had been cut badly and I was rushed to the nearest hospital. Although the procedure was uneventful, I had felt strangely sick coming out of the anesthetic and told the anesthesiologist so.

A few days later, I was informed that X-rays revealed I had a hernia that might prove troublesome if not quickly repaired. "No problem," I thought. And when the anesthesiologist who had supervised the first procedure informed me that he would also be sedating me during the hernia repair, I felt delighted.

"You'll be sure that nasty business with the anesthesia doesn't happen again, right?" I asked.

He nodded. "Not a chance, Jeanette. Since we now know that what we gave you last time caused a problem, we'll make a point to use something else. Something completely different. Most people don't realize there are over 150 different ways of compounding general anesthetic. If one's troublesome, we go to another that's chemically distinct." His gentle smile and tough, chiseled features presented a picture of calm confidence.

"Okay," I replied, still a bit shaky. "If you say so, then I guess it's fine."

He patted me on the shoulder with a quiet air of doctorliness, banishing my fears at once. "It *is* fine. And you'll be fine, too. The whole procedure will be just like a short rest. You'll wake up feeling terrific. I promise."

A short rest was exactly what I needed! The words had an almost magical effect. I felt a burning sensation as the doctor administered an injection. I mentioned the fact immediately, but was told the feeling was perfectly normal, that everything was okay. A pleasant drowsiness stole over my body like warm bath water. From the corner of my eye, I noticed that the anesthesiologist and nurse stood talking and laughing in a far corner. As aides wheeled me down a spotless corridor to the operating room, he and the nurse, in nonstop chatter, accompanied my gurney every step of the way. My thoughts moved with the heaviness of molasses: "I wonder how he can change the anesthetic if he's so busy talking. I wonder how..."

When they placed the mask over my face, I remembered saying hesitantly: "You guys better take good care of me. Remember, my daughters are counting on you. I love you. God bless you. I'll see you later." Then there was a loud ringing in my ears and I passed out.

Soon after I could hear people talking and thought how little time the procedure took. At the time I tried to swallow and realized the surgery wasn't over and in fact it hadn't even begun!

I told myself to remain calm and thought that maybe the doctors had done something different.

"I was wondering where you were." The anesthesiologist's query bit the cool antiseptic-laden atmosphere. Someone else had loudly pushed open the swinging doors of the operating room. I knew it had to be the surgeon.

"Sorry I'm late. The last case tore open. Had to stitch him up twice. What a hassle."

The utter incongruity of my situation was hitting home. My brain cried out: "Hey! Shouldn't I be asleep or something?" But try as I might, my

13

They were about to operate— even though I was fully conscious!

lips didn't even twitch, let alone release my protest. An icy-cold shudder passed down the full length of my body. "Hey! Over here! Don't I need some more anesthetic? I think something might be wrong!"

No one heard my thoughts, nor did they appear to know that I was even capable of them. My arms were stretched out and felt strapped down at right angles to my body. I tried to flex them, to flail out, but my muscles refused to respond with even so much as a slight movement.

"Give me the marker," said the surgeon, his fingers pushing and probing my lower abdomen. Soon his hand was replaced by a soft felt-tip pen moving obliquely in a razor-straight line, where the first incision would be made. Now I had no doubts whatsoever about precisely what was occurring. They were about to operate—even though I was fully conscious!

Panicked, I began to cry hysterically, trapped inside the prison of my own skull. In the back of my mind, I still believed that at least one person in the room would realize this terrible mistake at the last second. I remembered how, long ago in my parents' home, I watched an Alfred Hitchcock drama in which a man who had been paralyzed in an accident kept himself from being locked into a morgue's cold storage by weeping. His tears had given away the truth.

I wanted it to be the same with me, so I let myself go completely. And I wept, all right—mentally! But there was no sensation of moist drops flowing from my eyes. My cheeks remained bone-dry.

"Scalpel," said the surgeon to the nurse.

"Please don't!" my brain yelled out wildly to emptiness. "You can't do this! For God's sake, stop! Stop!"

At that instant, the surgeon's electric knife, which cuts and cauterizes

14

simultaneously, tore into my skin. It felt like a blowtorch. Lightning bolts of pain more intense than any pain I had ever experienced surged and ricocheted through my torso, finally exploding through the left side of my face. Drowning in an ocean of searing agony, I sensed the skein of my entire life unraveling, thread by thread. But I was the only one who heard my own tortured screams—silent screams that reverberated again and again off the cold walls of my skull and into the black night of eternity.

What had I done to deserve this punishment? I was only 34, but the beautiful regularities of my everyday life now appeared infinitely remote. I had always tried to live a decent life. Brought up Catholic, one of seven children, I never took much interest in the sciences or medicine. Doctors impressed me as serious, scholarly, and responsible. But I always enjoyed dealing with happy events and people, and so was fascinated with entertainment and the media. When I was very young, I was so quiet that my schoolmates teased me.

But I rapidly grew out of that; my teen years were full of activities. Boys sought me out because I was thin and attractive, and I reveled in the attention. In my early 30s I traveled to Texas and, almost at once, secured a series of good jobs in runway modeling as well as teaching and producing in the TV commercial business.

Whether showing off thousand-dollar designer creations on the runway to hundreds of gawking spectators and photographers or modeling casual outfits at small, informal get-togethers, my employers could always count on me to be cheerful and breezy. I loved what I did and it showed. I was proud of the fact that I could earn a good living in such a glamorous profession but I naturally kept an eye out for more significant challenges that might come my way. When the opportunity arrived for me to break into TV production work, I jumped at the chance. Meanwhile, my two girls were a source of endless joy. In short, I was no different than hundreds

15

There was a flash of white light and I found myself in two places at once: lying pale and broken on the operating table and, inexplicably, standing at my doctor's left side looking on impassively at the scene being played out. Behind me, I could sense the presence of an eerie brightness that I did not want to look at or even think about.

of thousands of other lucky, plucky American women. Until this...

My surreal anguish continued unabated. I could smell the nauseating stench of my own burning flesh as the electric scalpel continued to carve its way through inch after inch of skin and stomach muscles. To make matters worse, the air was filled with the sound of my body ripping open. I mentally screamed with all my might, but of course, no one in the operating room could hear me. The drugs and endotracheal tube in my throat prevented any sound I tried to make from being heard by anyone but me. Above the racket in my head, I heard the surgeon and anesthesiologist exchange coarse laughter at an obscene joke. The searing blade carved a path toward my head and deeper into my abdomen, hitting a nerve.

I felt as if two buckets of molten lead had smashed straight down below my collar bones, shattering everything beneath into a bloody pulp. My breath was being squeezed flat, like a small balloon crushed in a press, and somehow, I clearly understood that death was approaching.

There was a flash of white light and I found myself in two places at once: lying pale and broken on the operating table and, inexplicably, standing at my doctor's left side looking on impassively at the scene being played out. Behind me, I could sense the presence of an eerie brightness that I did not want to look at or even think about.

I stood outside of myself and prayed, "God, I know it's not my

16

time and my work here is not done and my daughters need me, so please God honor my free will and let me stay!"

In the next instant, I was back in my body on the table in severe pain, but I knew I would live if I could just hold on a little longer.

For the first time that day the anesthesiologist was troubled. "Hold it!" The vital-signs monitor kept on beeping like a broken alarm clock. "I want to give her another shot, okay?"

The cursed knife stopped. When that awful cutting ceased, some of my normal reasoning powers returned but the dawning comprehension of what was occurring, the knowledge that I was *not* having a nightmare or a hallucination, proved worse than the physical torture itself. To me, it was as if that red-hot knife had been ripping through my flesh for eons. My intellect reeled at the thought of the living hell I had entered. "How much more will come?" I thought numbly. "How much more can I stand before I go insane...or die?" A needle jabbed into my upper arm and I noticed a bit of relief in my chest. But I was still completely awake and in terrible pain.

The surgeon sounded irritated. "She's fine. Fifteen minutes and I'll be finished. What's the problem?"

"Yeah," the anesthesiologist muttered, apparently confused by the readings on his various monitors. "Yeah, I guess it's alright. Go ahead. You know, this babe's got great breasts."

"And how!" the surgeon agreed. "She doesn't need any of that silicone stuff, that's for sure."

And the howling agony began again, fully as intense as before, perhaps even worse. My wretched screaming that only I could hear had, to me, already acquired the frightening resonance of stark raving madness. More than anything, I wanted an end to it all; I wanted out. The option of death, which up to that point seemed hateful, now began to take on an

Help me, God! I don't have the strength to stay alive on my own anymore! Oh God, if I die, who will ever know I was awake?

aura of profound attractiveness; deep inside I understood that if I really sought it, I could take it. Moment by grinding moment, death's desirability grew. I became infatuated with the certainty that death would, without question, end my misery.

But was death the only way out? "Fifteen minutes," I groaned to the darkness over and over like a crazy woman chanting to a padded cell. "Only fifteen more minutes. I can make it. Fifteen minutes." Then, realizing that I was treading across some kind of narrow, ragged edge, I tried to pray. "Oh God, I don't want to find death. Don't allow me to make that choice. Even if it's the only way to stop the pain, I don't want to die! I have two loving and beautiful daughters. If I die, who'll look after them? I'm all my girls have. They're still so young. They'll suffer if I'm gone. I'm not begging for me but for them. Even if I've done something wrong, they're innocent. Please God, don't force me to leave now! Help me, God! I don't have the strength to stay alive on my own anymore! Oh God, if I die, who will ever know I was awake?"

Another gap, a pause in the hellish terror. "Well, I'll be damned," said the surgeon. "Look at this thing, will you? It's not a hernia. Just some fatty tissue. All that for nothing. This was really a waste of time."

Trying my best to hold on to a shred of good sense, to cling to the tiniest bit of everyday reason and morality, I shouted: "Shut up! Don't talk about me that way, damn you! Why don't you pay attention to what you're doing? I'm a human being! Same as you! I'm a person. I *am* somebody. I'm my mother and father's daughter and Lisa and Valerie's mom. How can you talk to another living, breathing, feeling human being that way? How dare you?" But trapped in my own head, I was only yelling to myself.

The surgeon spoke: "Well. End of the line. I'm stitching her up. Give me a syringe with some Novocaine."

"Why are you giving her Novocaine?" asked the nurse.

"Stops them from complaining about the cut. Works like a charm. For a day, anyway."

The nurse chuckled. "Some of them would complain if you hit them over the head with a baseball bat."

When his needle shot into the hole in my stomach, there was no relief, only more pain. I bellowed once more with all the energy I could muster, still saying nothing. And I kept on silently screaming with each and every penetrating stitch and pull, right to the last.

"Get her out of here," ordered the surgeon.

The nurse was on my left side, and when she pulled off the grounding plate it felt like my flesh was pulled off with it.

Then, with a wrenching snap, the nurse tried to take out the catheter. I thought every stitch had torn open. She laughed, saying, "Oh, I forgot to deflate the damn thing!" Finally, she ripped something off my left thigh that made me scream inside as she hollered, "She's ready to go."

As the anesthesiologist hoisted my torso from the armpits, the surgeon grabbed my legs. Together, they swung me off the table like a sack of potatoes and dropped me onto a gurney. For an instant, I thought: "My God, how can they treat me like this after what I've been through. I thought they're supposed to treat you gently in a hospital." When I thumped down hard, a tremendous pain shot across my side and I began screaming again. Still, no one heard. As I was wheeled into recovery, I desperately wanted to reach down and hold the gash, which hurt so badly, but my arms remained immobile, like pieces of wood.

A woman's voice was calling into my ear: "Wake up, hon! You're in the recovery room. Time to wake up!"

Her Giorgio perfume pervaded the place as she called out to me at short intervals again and again. But I still couldn't move or even open my eyes. At first I yelled in reply, "I'm awake! I never went to sleep! Why can't you see that?" But still my voice was trapped deep within my skull. Then I became even more frightened.

I thought, "I'm in a coma! Maybe I'm dead and in Hell! But why? Why me of all people? May God have mercy on my soul."

Reflecting endlessly on the vain struggle I had waged in the operating room, my still-imprisoned consciousness writhed much the way an impaled worm squirms vainly on a fishhook. My whole body ached as if I had run miles uphill. The place where the electric knife had slit my abdomen was so sore I feared it would rip open, spilling my innards onto the polished floor. Would I ever get out of this living nightmare?

Finally, panting and gasping like a drowning person coming up for air one last time, I felt a significant change. My consciousness was moving into my limbs and face, taking up its familiar place once more. I was no longer trapped inside my head! I tried to wiggle a finger—it responded!

My arm shifted. It was true; I was back among the living again! But as soon as I gained my freedom, my body started to shake violently. The nurse yelled for help and people ran to my bedside, holding me down. People were asking me what was wrong. I was wrapped up like a mummy with only a tiny hole for my face. At that time, the only thing I could do was shriek and cry and say over and over again: "I was awake! I was awake!"

"How are you feeling, hon?" the Giorgio-soaked nurse continued to croon obnoxiously. "You're doing just fine. The operation went great and the doctors say…"

"What are you talking about?" I rasped. The emotions I experienced then were so utterly overwhelming I could feel my eyes bulge from their sockets.

"I'm not doing fine! It wasn't great! I felt everything! They almost killed me! Do you hear me? I was awake! Awake every second. Every damn second!"

The nurse's eyes narrowed. "Now, hon, you know you were asleep. You had a bad dream, that's all. Lots of patients have them. You may think that you felt something but…"

I tried to sit up but the pain in my abdomen stabbed through me like a flaming arrow. Sucking in my breath, I fell back heavily onto the mattress.

"Hey, don't move around yet. You wouldn't want to pull those stitches loose now, would you?"

A geyser of rage welled up from deep within. "What the hell do you care? They just operated on me like a goddam piece of meat! I felt everything—everything. Now you think you can treat me like a naughty child, put me in the corner and…"

The nurse said, "You must stop this or you can't go back to your room."

They wheeled me to a room where some of my friends were anxiously waiting. Immediately, I told them to call my family physician, the last among that professional fraternity whom I still trusted. Within a few minutes he arrived at the hospital.

As soon as he saw me, he exclaimed, "My God! Tell me what happened!" I managed to blurt out the whole experience before becoming hysterical again.

That evening I was moved to a private room. No one spoke to me or even came near and I was overcome by the feeling that I had done something terribly wrong. Anger must have shown on my face when the anesthesiologist suddenly showed up that evening.

His eyes shifted nervously around the room before retracing their path to my bed. "Jeanette, is something the matter? I understand you think you were awake during your surgery."

I angrily replied, "Yeah, there's something the matter! I was awake the whole time! It hurt like hell! How come you didn't notice? How could you do something like that? I was wide awake!"

A smile flickered across his face. "No, Jeanette. You were dreaming."

"I wasn't!" I shrieked at the top of my lungs.

"Yes, you were. It happens sometimes." With measured cadence, he continued. "Control yourself, please. Don't jump to conclusions before you've heard what I have to say. All clinical indications showed you were completely unconscious. Anesthetics can cause very vivid dreams once in a while. Usually you sleep deeply. But on occasion, you might dream a lot. Bad dreams. Where you might imagine you felt or heard things that didn't really occur. Anesthetic sleep can produce some unusual effects. Strange dreams can seem real. Maybe that's what happened to you, Jeanette."

"It's not!" I exclaimed.

He responded, "You've got to relax. Take some time to think about what I've said. You're upset now. Believe me, I understand. You still can't think clearly."

I declared, "I can think straight enough to remember what you said about my breasts. And all the other rotten remarks, too. Is that part of your professional training?"

The anesthesiologist's mouth dropped open. He looked like a frightened child, and then said, "What can I do? I'll do anything."

"Fine," I replied. "How about you and I go back to that operating room. Let me put you on that table and paralyze your whole body but keep you awake. And the surgeon can do a hernia repair on you that you don't need. How's that? Okay?"

I broke down and started to sob pitifully. He gently touched my shoulders but the tears refused to stop. Visibly shaken, he walked out.

The next morning, it was the surgeon's turn to visit. His presence provoked an immediate challenge from me, and I demanded, "Tell me what you did in that operating room! What was wrong with me? I want you to tell me exactly why I needed the operation."

The surgeon pulled at his left ear, and hedged, "What I did? Well, we did what we set out to do. Naturally. You had a hernia. We repaired it."

My fists clenched into tight knots. "You're lying," I hissed. "There was no hernia. You took out a piece of fatty tissue. Isn't that what you did? There was no hernia! The whole operation was a waste of time! That's what you said."

I watched the surgeon shudder and turn pale. "Jesus, I only do the surgery," he muttered. "How am I supposed to know if you're out or not?"

"You should save your patients' money instead of giving them those stupid Novocaine shots. They don't work!"

In the pall of silence that had descended, he quickly turned and almost ran from the room. A nurse eyed me balefully, obviously at a surprising loss for words, her discomfort written large.

That afternoon I saw my personal physician and a psychologist. I told them I no longer felt safe in the hospital, that all I wanted was to go home and be with my children. They agreed but told me that for medical reasons I had to remain there for one more night.

"Please," I pleaded, "leave the door and curtains open and the lights on. I'm terrified of this place. I don't want to be left alone again in the dark." They promised to respect my wishes.

"Don't say a word," she whispered. "If they find out I'm here, I'm good as fired."

"Why?" I asked softly.

She said, "Because when something like this—somebody like you—happens, they don't want it spread around. They treat it like it's your fantasy, you know? That's why you're here, isolated from the rest of the staff."

I was placed in a private room. As darkness deepened, I began to feel afraid. The events of the day rushed back so I was unable to sleep, but I refused medication that would have knocked me out. In the evening silence, incredible paranoid notions filtered into my seething brain: What if the doctors wanted to shut me up for good to protect their reputations?

Feeling increasingly imprisoned and imperiled, I seriously entertained the notion of bolting from the hospital. It was about then that an unfamiliar nurse, a woman in her early 40s, entered the room. She held a forefinger to her lips.

"Don't say a word," she whispered. "If they find out I'm here, I'm good as fired."

"Why?" I asked softly.

She said, "Because when something like this—somebody like you—happens, they don't want it spread around. They treat it like it's your fantasy, you know? That's why you're here, isolated from the rest of the staff."

"Am I in danger?" I queried.

She emphatically replied, "Oh no! They just want you out of their hair as soon as possible. And they hope to God you won't sue."

I was amazed but relieved, and asked, "You mean this has happened before?"

The woman smiled and said, "Oh, yes. A bunch of times. Once..."

Before she could finish, we heard shuffling sounds in the hall outside that announced the imminent arrival of the night nurse who had previously attempted to dispense sleeping pills to me. "Don't say a word, okay?" breathed the woman as she vanished into the bathroom.

As the figure of the night nurse loomed up, I could hear the curtain pulled around the bathtub.

"Still awake?" queried the pill-toting woman curtly.

"Yes. I had a rough day," I quietly replied.

"Why don't you take some of these?" she insisted.

"No, thank you," I firmly replied.

Her eyes made a cursory survey of the small, square chamber, and asked, "Were you talking to somebody?"

"What? Who?" I lied. "Nobody but you has come up here. It's as quiet as a grave."

The nurse made a suspicious face and said, "Okay. Good night."

I added, "If I fall asleep, please don't forget to leave the door open and the lights on."

There was no acknowledgment of my request. As she left, she turned back briefly at the doorway to look around once more, as if she thought someone might materialize out of the woodwork. I listened to her shuffling steps fading away down the long corridor.

My guest immediately reappeared, but only for a moment to say, "I've got to go now. God bless you." Then she was gone.

Exhausted, I finally fell asleep. But my dreams were warped beyond imagining, and when I awoke after a few restless hours, the door was shut, the curtains were closed and all the lights were out. The four walls turned blood-red and seemed to press in on me. I was trapped—again!

Horrifying nightmares are my companions when others slumber peacefully...

Immediately my breath became labored. I struggled for air. For a second time, I smelled my own burning flesh and I shriveled beneath the onslaught of the merciless scalpel. Hysterically, I grabbed for the light and almost fell out of bed.

The next day I checked out of the hospital and went home. But the memory of what occurred there still haunts me 12 years later. Since then I haven't been the same person. Sometimes I feel a cosmic hollowness, as if my soul has left my body and can't return. Sleeping or waking, I still involuntarily experience the operating room torments. Horrifying nightmares are my companions when others slumber peacefully, often shocking me wide awake. But when my eyes pop open there is still no respite because the walls and ceiling turn blood-red. For a long time I was afraid to go to bed without a night light, and the blinds had to be left open.

I used to smell Giorgio perfume when no one is there, and could not drive at night or at rush hour for many years. Remembering the simplest things, like how to get to the airport or spell a word, was often difficult and sometimes impossible.

That day my whole life changed. But now, at least, I know for certain my experience was not unique. Sadly, it can still happen, even today.

CHAPTER 2

A PROBLEM WITHOUT A NAME
"...the invisible scars of surgery."

ince the beginning of anesthesia's widespread use, providers have encountered flaws in its supposedly seamless fabric of oblivion.

That may seem shocking, but we really have no reason to be surprised. The fact is anesthesia is no more or less than any other powerful and pervasive technology, and no technology operates perfectly all the time. It makes no difference that anesthesia deals directly with the issue of human pain.

Like other technologies in which we put our faith, anesthesia's problems match its level of sophistication.

Like other technologies in which we put our faith, anesthesia's problems match its level of sophistication. All engineers understand that the more complicated a system is, the more likely it is to malfunction at some-

The very notion that anesthesia might not work each and every time exactly the way it's intended carries a note of horror that reverberates loudly above any ordinary problems encountered with modern technology.

time or another. The history of anesthesia has been one where scientific advancements are often uneven and never totally complete. Occasionally, this uneven advancement can leave surprising flaws in the technology.

When we plunk down a large chunk of our hard-earned money for an automobile, we take tire and engine problems for granted even though life and limb may be put at stake when blowouts or stalls occur. We confidently purchase airline tickets for business and pleasure even though news reports occasionally show grisly on-the-scene footage of airplane crashes or train wrecks. Glitches are common in our phone service even while business and social affairs have come to depend completely on words and figures zipping from place to place at the speed of sound and light.

In each and every one of our highly complex technologies, we take the possibility of failure for granted. We understand that breakdowns and breakups are part and parcel of modern life; they're the price we're forced to pay for receiving large benefits from our miraculous devices. But we balk at the thought that the chemicals, machines, and experts that insulate us from pain in the operating room are also susceptible to failure. The very notion that anesthesia might not work each and every time exactly the way it's intended carries a note of horror that reverberates loudly above any ordinary problems encountered with modern technology.

Perhaps this attitude is not so difficult to fathom. It may well be due to an intuitive realization that a few minutes of surgery with only an illusion of anesthesia might be quite a bit worse than simply shuffling off this mortal coil. As we will see later, that idea is not so far from the truth.

Instinctive revulsion at the thought that the doors of consciousness might, without warning, swing open on the operating table is so powerful that it affects anesthesia providers and patients alike. The common human instinct to turn away from something that is particularly awful is always at work.

Basically, that type of instinct serves to protect us but it also carries the potential to blind us to important truths. Human progress in both the arts and sciences is determined by our willingness—or unwillingness—to look closely and honestly at baffling and unpleasant realities.

In spite of the fact that some information about anesthesia awareness existed, for a long time it was not seen as important in the big picture of medical practice. Of course, nothing could be further from the truth for those patients who experience awareness. The technology of medicine can be so intense that some of the gaps in that technology get ignored. Some in medicine are loath to dwell on those missing gaps, preferring to pursue the next technological miracle. This pursuit of technology can blind providers to the weak points in that technological armor for fear of losing prestige and the public trust. Doctors suffer not so much from insensitivity as from good old-fashioned anxiety—anxiety about maintaining professional respect and authority, and anxiety about their all-too-human status. They are critically aware that everyday technological foul-ups like power outages and computer viruses are nothing compared to minutes or hours of raw agony and mind-wrenching pain. However, they did not give this problem the attention it needed for too long.

For their part, patients simply prefer not to think about such frightening problems—they are content to ignore them out of existence. Most view surgery as a necessity that is harrowing enough. Physically compromised and in need of help, patients desperately want to believe that by trusting the medical experts, everything is bound to come out all right.

How can we blame them for wanting to look only at the bright side of things? I was in exactly the same position myself, once upon a time.

What's worse, however, is that anesthesia's occasional failure to obtund consciousness invariably goes unrecognized until it is too late. Consciousness itself has no color or texture or smell. Although it lies at the very core of our being, it can only be perceived by others if we give behavioral evidence of its presence in observable actions or audible sounds. When medical technology removes our powers to move and speak, to make our bodies conform with our wills, consciousness floats alone on an uncharted sea, carried along by mysterious currents we barely understand even today. Like a shipwrecked sailor adrift on a log, consciousness minus deeds and words is an invisible, undetectable speck lost in a vast nothingness. Although such images seem melodramatic, they accurately convey the devastating isolation of a patient who "comes to" during an operation, and who is the only person aware of the situation.

When a boiler explodes or a ship springs a leak, a distress cry goes out at once and help is dispatched. But when a patient prematurely recovers consciousness, no one else can feel, let alone intervene in, the shocking tragedy that then unfolds step by merciless step.

What we all must understand is that like other technological wonders, anesthesia will never be perfect. The greater problem is this: Because anesthesia is so wonderful when it works as it usually does, few have the courage to speak out when it fails.

Throughout the history of anesthesia and right up to the present, many anesthesia researchers and providers have refused to accept or have significantly downplayed the reality of anesthetic awareness. The result: Those patients who partially awaken from anesthesia's chemical embrace find themselves more alone than they will probably ever be in their entire lives.

To understand why this is so, it is necessary to review the history of

what the medical profession calls anesthetic awareness, or what happens when consciousness unex-
pectedly intrudes on anesthetic-induced sleep in
the operating room.

Anesthetic awareness is literally as old as the
practice of anesthesia itself but has always been relegated to the back pages of medical journals and
thus the periphery of medical concern. Touting
anesthesia's success brings confidence to doctors
and patients alike, but dwelling on its failures is
depressing and often terrifying.

Touting anesthesia's
success brings con-
fidence to doctors
and patients alike,
but dwelling on
its failures is
depressing and
often terrifying.

Reports of severe pain during anesthesia emerged simultaneously
with the first tentative uses of the technique during the mid-19th century.
But this shattering fact remained shrouded in a cloud of secrecy, to be con-
templated privately by a handful of specialists and academics.

As early as 1846, a woman who had apparently undergone an
uneventful surgery under nitrous oxide at Massachusetts General Hospital
subsequently reported that she felt every detail of the procedure from beginning to end. Describing her torment in vivid detail that the presiding physicians recognized as an accurate account, she noted how "the noise of sawing
wood" accompanied the back-and-forth motion of a bone saw and compared
the stabbing, tearing pain she experienced to a "reaping hook in her arm."

Nitrous oxide was recognized as an incomplete anesthetic and the
search for improvement was launched. Not until the 1940s were some professionals beginning to understand that some anesthesia techniques could
produce a body that would lie still for the surgeon's knife, but was not
always unconscious. Great strides in techniques and drugs were made, giving the medical profession the false assurance that technology had solved
the problem encountered in 1846 at Massachusetts General.

There is no question that physician denial is the single biggest obstacle not only to progress in anesthesia awareness technology but also to helping patients who have endured anesthetic awareness and are trying to cope with the reality of the living nightmares into which they have been catapulted.

Techniques and knowledge were vastly improved. Failure did not seem likely from a technical viewpoint. Many doctors dismissed awareness under anesthesia with a smile and a shrug. Many still tell the panicked victims of awareness that they "have deep-rooted psychological problems" or they "were having a bad dream." There is no question that physician denial is the single biggest obstacle not only to progress in anesthesia awareness technology but also to helping patients who have endured anesthetic awareness and are trying to cope with the reality of the living nightmares into which they have been catapulted.

The year 1950 marked a momentous turning point in the acknowledgment of anesthetic awareness. It was then that Dr. E.H. Winterbottom coined a new phrase in the prestigious *British Medical Journal,* "the invisible scars of surgery."[1] His sensitive words marked the first specific historical reference to the immense psychological trauma caused by anesthetic awareness. It was the first time a recognized medical authority admitted a serious problem with anesthesia. Although the skeleton of anesthetic awareness had, at long last, been dragged out of its closet, most physicians still persisted in turning away. For the most part, the phenomenon was considered too rare to be of concern or too insignificant for scientific attention.

Approximately five years after Winterbottom's landmark report, however, a few physicians began to offer statistical evidence to the contrary.

Then, in 1976, an editorial in the *British Medical Journal* revealed that, overall, cases where consciousness erupted through anesthesia could reach as high as 25 percent.[2] As reports came into the literature, patients whose lives were shattered by awareness experiences were increasingly willing to take their cases not only to the psychiatrist's couch but also to court. Needless to say, their efforts to secure reasonable monetary compensation for incredible pain and suffering immediately caught the attention of organizations providing surgical malpractice insurance.

Because consciousness is invisible and impalpable, anesthesia providers have relied on various groups of signs that generally correlate with the presence of active awareness and the perception of pain. Of course, the operative term here is "generally," as a lack of physiological indication invariably accompanies anesthetic awareness in every circumstance.

Three principal levels of anesthetic "depth" were first defined in 1847. The descriptions offered then were vague, broad, and dependent on testimony that could only be given after the fact. Thus, there was much built-in leeway for error or misinterpretation in these descriptions: "The first stage is a pleasurable feeling of half intoxication; the second one, one of extreme pleasure; and the third stage, one of profound intoxication and insensibility."[3]

Surgical procedures were supposed to be started only at the final stage. But how could doctors hope to know what was going on inside a patient's head? In the final analysis, the old list of stages simply replaced one unknown—the degree of consciousness present—with several others equally obscure. The language sounded scientific, but the practice was far from it.

That same year, the purely subjective interpretation of stages was replaced by a series of physical signs like heart rate, respiration depth, and pupil diameter.[4] Although these were not strictly quantitative, at least they provided a set of somewhat more meaningful guidelines to let anesthesia providers know whether surgeons could begin invasive procedures.

From the 1920s onward, defects in matching the traditional signs to levels of consciousness and problems with interpretation of the signs themselves led to a new standard that augmented or replaced the others. Skeletal muscle activity came into vogue as the basic means for judging anesthetic depth. It, too, appeared reasonably scientific and practical. Evidence to the contrary was quickly shunted aside into the dusty drawer of anecdote and aberration.

But as more and more anesthetics came into popular use in the operating room, accurate and timely interpretation of these supposedly definitive signs became ever more difficult and subjective. Each anesthetic agent produced its own unique complex of signs and no two were alike.

When a specific list of signs was added to those produced by auxiliary medications such as opiates, anesthetic depth became progressively harder to gauge accurately, even for healthcare professionals familiar with the way the agents worked. If a less serious field of knowledge was involved, the situation might well be considered humorous: operating room technology had become so sophisticated that it was running perilously far ahead of itself.

In addition, it was difficult to calculate the patient's own unique physical and mental condition into all of these equations. Sensitivity to anesthesia often varies with age, disease, nature of the operation, and so on. Once again, the signs would change according to each patient's treatment schedule and problems. Charts, graphs, and math can only bring understanding so far, especially when consciousness is the issue in question. Consciousness is not a simple chemical reaction: It is too unique a phenomenon to respond exactly on cue every time.

But undoubtedly, the one factor that was most responsible for muddying the waters of anesthetic technology was the introduction in the 1940s of muscle relaxants like curare.[5] Heralded as the dawn of a safer era of anesthesia, these powerful agents soon proved to be double-edged swords.

There was good reason to bring muscle relaxants into the operating room initially. Anesthetics of the day, such as ether, were potent chemicals that could produce long-lasting results. Patients would sleep for hours after surgery, and retching nausea often lasted for hours after awakening. Some of the side effects of these drugs included potential damage to the liver or kidneys. Doctors realized that combining muscle relaxants with lower doses of anesthetics could lessen these problems. Greater muscle relaxation provided the surgeon with a better operating field, increasing their precision and decreasing the time needed to do some operations. As muscle relaxants decreased the ability to breathe, machines or ventilators were also used, while small, precisely controlled doses of anesthetic were administered to maintain unconsciousness. The patients were exposed to less of the sometimes toxic drugs, the surgeon had an improved operating field, and the patient's vital signs were more stable. However, the relaxants virtually wiped out the usefulness of skeletal muscle activity as an indication of anesthetic depth.

Given the complicated physiological profiles generated by the huge number of available anesthetics, muscle activity had become the crucial factor for any meaningful assessment of awareness. When things worked right in the now narrower tolerance of the operating room—and they usually did—patients awoke sooner, sounder, and happier than ever before. But when things went wrong, the operating room had the potential to resemble a torture chamber, minus only the screams of the victims. Reports of anesthetic awareness began to increase alarmingly as curare and its muscle-relaxant cousins were established as a normal part of operating room technique. That trend has continued up to the present day because not enough has been done to change it.

There are two distinct types of awareness that can occur under gen-

In reality, when it comes to judging whether consciousness is present on the operating table, anesthesia providers still lack an accurate, proven monitor of unconsciousness.

eral anesthesia: Anesthetic awareness with *explicit* recall and anesthetic awareness with *implicit* recall. (A short note for reader clarification: In a general anesthetic the patient is given medications that are expected to relieve the pain of the surgery *and* prevent consciousness. For some procedures, such as an endoscopy, the patient is given significant sedation, and may not remember any of the procedure, but total unconsciousness is not expected as it is in a general anesthetic. Additionally, there are types of regional and local anesthesia where it is not expected that the patient will be completely unconscious. A patient having a spinal anesthetic, for example, may be pain free for the surgery, have some sedation just for relaxation, and still remember parts of conversations or noises from the operation without experiencing pain. This is the expected result.)

Both types of anesthetic awareness form a continuum or spectrum of states. With explicit recall, memories can range from virtually every word and action of operating room personnel to only a few selected recollections. Explicit recall is responsible for the most traumatic and horrific incidents of anesthetic awareness, the ones that will receive the greatest attention in this book.

Implicit recall, on the other hand, can be an equally serious problem. Implicit recall emerges indirectly through painful, often inexplicable, psychological difficulties that appear following surgery. Often in these cases a few ill-spoken comments made by hospital staffers will subtly infiltrate the unconscious, producing vague yet adverse effects on self-image and lifestyle.

Since the increased reporting of anesthetic awareness incidents in the latter half of the 20th century, some doctors have been working to establish newer, more effective indexes of consciousness. For example, brain wave measurements were initially thought to provide the answer. However, no reliable correlation between brain waves and consciousness could be found, despite use of the most sophisticated computerized analyzers. In reality, when it comes to judging whether consciousness is present on the operating table, anesthesia providers still lack an accurate, proven monitor of unconsciousness. Absolute control over patient consciousness remains elusive. When consciousness manifests at unsuitable times and places, patient lives can be inadvertently put at risk and quite frequently psychologically destroyed.

REFERENCES

1. Winterbottom EH. Insufficient anaesthesia. *BJM*. 1950;1:247-248.

2. Awareness during anaesthesia [editorial]. *Br. Med J.* 1976;1:977.

3. Plomley F. Operation upon the eye. *Lancet.* 1847;1:134-135.

4. Snow J. A lecture on the inhalation of vapour of ether in surgical operations. *Lancet.* 1847;1:551-554.

5. Thatcher VS. *History of Anesthesia With Emphasis on the Nurse Specialist.* Philadelphia, Pa: JB Lippincott; 1953:174-175.

CHAPTER 3

A Living Testimony
"...nothing could possibly go wrong."

or too long the medical establishment has downplayed or ignored anesthetic awareness by burying it beneath a welter of cold statistics and clinical terminology. Medical journals were known to dismiss the subject by noting that awareness under anesthesia can be emotionally distressing to patients and advising physicians to maintain a professional demeanor if a patient reports recalling events during surgery.

Medical journals were known to dismiss the subject by noting that awareness under anesthesia can be emotionally distressing to patients...

As long as those responsible for administering anesthesia downplay and defuse the human agony resulting from the failure of anesthetics, people will continue to suffer needlessly. Moreover, those who have suffered will have done so in vain. Only when anesthesia providers, surgeons, and hospital administrators can look straight into the human face of anesthetic awareness

Her experience of being awake during surgery turned the course of her life down a dark and frightening road.

will they be able to grapple with it intelligently.

Thousands of detailed accounts of anesthetic awareness are available, with more coming to light everyday as awareness patients realize the importance of sharing their experiences with the public. Deborah, who was a victim of awareness, tells a harrowing account of her ordeal. Her experience of being awake during surgery turned the course of her life down a dark and frightening road. This is the rule for such incidents, not the exception. Deborah's name has been changed to protect her privacy and allow ongoing litigation. This is her story.

DEBORAH

I always had great faith in doctors, all doctors. I appreciated their training and the heavy responsibilities laid on them by their profession. I had to because I worked with them from 9 to 5 everyday as an administrative secretary.

Before my last operation—the bad one, the nightmare—I went through four others. None caused any problems. There was no reason to believe this time would be any different. Funny how wrong you can be.

Before the incident my life was great. My childhood was an incredibly happy one. When I was a kid, my brothers and sisters and I often volunteered in a Polish-American rest home. We'd push wheelchair-bound patients to church on Sundays and Christmas. No one forced us; we enjoyed being helpful. In the rest home, I received my first lengthy exposure to the medical profession and it was very positive. When the time came for me to think about a career those memories proved decisive.

The doctors weren't sure if I had a hernia. Previously, exercise after having a baby had brought on some bouts of tendinitis in my groin. So

40

they wanted to go in and look around a bit and handle any minor problems they might run across. I knew each one of those doctors personally. I hand-picked them for the job. I thought they were my friends, that they would never do anything to hurt me. In my work, people would come to me for advice on putting surgical teams together. All the time I'd hear, "Oh Deborah, you arrange that stuff so well. You're so detailed. You understand who's best at what. You always think of everything."

I hand-picked them for the job. I thought they were my friends, that they would never do anything to hurt me.

I thought the doctors were going to take care of me; that I was one of them. So I was confident that nothing could possibly go wrong.

My husband dropped me off at the hospital the night before. He asked me if I was worried, if I wanted him to be there, but I told him he was being silly. "You'd worry about having a tooth filled. What could possibly happen?" I said. "I'll see you at noon tomorrow."

Right before the surgery I was laying on a gurney in the hall. I wanted to say a few words to the anesthesiologist and the surgeon before the procedure started—nothing earthshaking, just how I felt. But I never got the chance. All of a sudden the anesthesiologist was injecting something into me through a catheter. "Hello! Hi!" I piped.

"I'm giving you some medicine," he answered. He was quite brusque, as if he was rushed and didn't want to be bothered.

I thought he was giving me an antibiotic or a local or something. Then the gurney began rolling down the hall and into the operating room. My eyes closed. I felt drowsy but never passed out. I expected to get the real anesthetic at anytime. Meanwhile, I knew exactly what was going on, I just couldn't see it. I felt chilly. The table was incredibly cold, like it had been in

I knew the anesthesiologist. I thought, "Where the hell is he? Why doesn't he pick up on this?" After I had begged and pleaded for a long time I started shaking. My head was hanging back and it began to tremble. The anesthesiologist must have seen it. He said, "Hey! Hey, give her more!"

a refrigerator. To make matters worse, I was in a very uncomfortable position. When I tried to say something about it, though, the words refused to come out. They put an electrical ground on my leg and some light blankets over me. They thought I was completely out. I still didn't understand that.

Nobody talked to me and I couldn't imagine why. "They're sure being rude," I thought. All at once I felt a huge needle shoved into my groin. I didn't know why they didn't make some remark about what was happening. Doctors always say stuff like, "You'll feel a little pinprick" or "It'll be over in a second." These are just things to put you more at ease. But they didn't give me any warning at all.

Then matters started to get out of hand. I could feel them pulling things out of me. And the metal clamps. Pain began to mount up. Soon it was excruciating. The most horrible part was that they were talking and laughing more and more as they went on. I tried to make myself heard. I was screaming in my head, "That hurts! You're hurting me! Stop!" But of course they couldn't hear me.

I started flipping out. I was begging them to stop. Their laughter only got louder. Soon things got too much to bear. The pain was awful. No one should be allowed to suffer like that. It's not human. I wanted to die, to commit suicide. I was pulling, tugging, writhing.

I knew the anesthesiologist. I thought, "Where the hell is he? Why doesn't he pick up on this?" After I had begged and pleaded for a long time

I started shaking. My head was hanging back and it began to tremble. The anesthesiologist must have seen it. He said, "Hey! Hey, give her more!"

The rest of them weren't listening because they were still chuckling about…I don't know what. But when he hollered it again there was dead silence.

Someone remarked, "Yeah, sorry. Let us know if it hurts."

"What the hell's the matter with you?" my mind screamed back. "I've been trying to tell you. What do you want me to do?" Two more needles were shoved into my groin. They felt just like daggers.

The anesthesiologist leaned over me and muttered, "I guess things didn't go exactly as they should have." Later, he denied ever making that remark.

I still believe I might have been able to take the pain if I had been prepared. But the whole business took me completely off guard.

I began to feel delirious. One thing got mixed up with another and all of them were spinning around. I can't remember anymore of what happened during the rest of the operation. I was told later that no problems were found. No hernia, no disease, nothing.

I snapped out of it as soon as they finished sewing me up. I was so completely awake that I sat up on the operating table, saw the gurney wheeled in, walked over to it, and laid down again.

At that point my condition was obvious to everyone. The anesthesiologist leaned over me and muttered, "I guess things didn't go exactly as they should have." Later, he denied ever making that remark.

They quickly wheeled me down the hall and into an area where they shut me behind some drapes. Everyone, all the nurses and aides, were silent. They looked at me strangely. I'd never seen such ominous looks

> *"No one would suspect anything if I died here."*

before. So I began to get scared, really scared.

I thought, "What just happened? If it ever got out, it might ruin the doctors and even the hospital. Suppose they want to make sure it never does? No one would suspect anything if I died here. No one would even bother to investigate. People die from operations all the time. And a physician would know exactly how to do the job, too." You might think I was being paranoid. But after what I just went through, it made perfect sense.

I told the nurse that I was ready to leave, that everything was fine. I didn't want to let on what I was thinking about. She told me I should go to the bathroom first. Immediately, I got to my feet and obeyed. I felt as if I was locked away in a brutal prison and a guard had given me an order. I didn't dare disobey. What I feared most was not being killed but being taken back and tortured again. Had they asked me to, I would have walked on the ceiling.

In the bathroom I was too frightened to relieve myself. Every muscle was tied in knots. So I turned on the water for a few minutes and held onto the steel railing. When I came out the nurse asked me, "Did you go?"

She suspected disobedience! "No!" I blurted out. "No, I couldn't."

Aides wheeled the bed away and I was made to sit in a recliner. By this time the post-operative pain was beginning to eat into me. When the nurse asked if I wanted some medication for it I refused. I was afraid of being knocked out, of being helpless while they put me to sleep forever or worked me over again.

I sat there, stock still, for hours. Although I was getting very tired, the last think I wanted was to fall asleep. My fear grew so strong I could almost touch it. All I wanted was to be let out, to go home where it was safe.

Finally, my husband showed up with our baby. I got dressed by

44

myself. Not realizing anything was wrong, he simply said, "Hi. How are you doing?"

At that moment an emotional dam broke
inside me. "Where the hell were you?" I screamed
at the top of my lungs. He went pale and pulled
back. "Let's go! Come on, let's go!" I bellowed.

"Let me get the car," he said softly. A thou-
sand years seemed to pass as I waited for him to
pull up to the front lobby.

We hadn't driven to the corner when I started
to yell again. "They were hurting me, dammit! They
hurt me bad! You wouldn't believe what they did to
me! It was so awful. And they couldn't even hear me
because they were laughing. Laughing!"

> *My husband looked at me out of the corner of his eye. The pleasant, cheerful wife he had always known was gone and now there was a mad-woman sitting beside him.*

My husband looked at me out of the corner of his eye. The pleasant,
cheerful wife he had always known was gone and now there was a mad-
woman sitting beside him. Uneasiness crept across his face. I didn't want to
talk to him any longer, so when I got home I went straight to bed even
though it was noon.

That was a Friday. For the rest of the weekend, whenever I saw my
husband I would start all over, trying to communicate the hell I had been
through. I believed I could make him understand. Nights were especially
bad. Every time I lay on my back it seemed I was on the operating table
again. I'd have to sit up and walk around and pull myself together. Finally,
I'd pass out from sheer exhaustion. I'd get up crying uncontrollably from
nightmares about unspeakable tortures. My husband would hold me, trying
to comfort me, but it simply didn't work. Because I didn't want to wake the
kids, I'd go to the living room to sob.

Things didn't improve. I slept only in short naps. When I talked to a neighbor, I always brought the conversation back to my operation, how they hurt me so badly, how they just laughed when I tried to cry out. I felt as though I'd been violated.

My husband suggested I call the anesthesiologist on Monday to straighten matters out. I agreed. But when the time came, I found I was too upset to call the hospital and begged my husband to do it. The anesthesiologist was out of town. Although I knew the surgeon was on call that weekend, he made no attempt to communicate with me. My husband left messages asking both of them to get in touch. Clearly, no one on the hospital staff cared about what had occurred or showed any interest in how I was doing. My inner turmoil grew. At my husband's suggestion I made an appointment to see a counselor. But that didn't help either. He didn't take my story seriously.

That week the surgeon's nurse phoned and I answered. She said, "Deborah, this is Marie from Dr. ___'s office. He heard you had some problems after the operation and wanted to say it's too bad."

I couldn't believe the insensitivity of her remark and I flew into a rage. " 'Too bad'! What do you mean 'too bad'? I didn't run my nylons or something! That's what you call 'too bad'? You better tell Dr. ___ to call my husband tomorrow and his story better be damned good."

"I'll tell you what," the nurse calmly replied. "I'll make an appointment for you to see the doctor tomorrow. You can talk to him yourself."

"No way!" I screamed back. The force of my own anger surprised me but I couldn't keep it down. "I don't intend to go anywhere near him."

At that time my husband had to leave town on business. Normally, this would have meant only a little inconvenience. I was a working woman who had functioned independently my whole adult life. But after the operation my confidence vanished. I found myself calling my husband about 10 times a day, seeking reassurance from him that he was okay, that everything was fine, that he'd be back soon. Again, I knew what I was doing. I understood how silly it was. But I was so fearful, so intimidated, that I couldn't stop. I was like a little girl running from shadows.

In the same way, I used to drive everywhere, sometimes visiting relatives eight hours away. Now my knees knocked together when I tried to drive. Not only was I desperately afraid of leaving the house for a minute, I'd check and recheck locks and windows. I'd clutch my little terrier, imagining that he'd go after anyone who'd want to harm me. So my thoughts and behavior degenerated until I was just a quivering shell.

Sensing now that a serious problem was developing, my husband asked his mother to stay with me. A few days later the phone rang. As soon as I heard the voice on the other end I knew who it was: the surgeon.

I yelled so loudly I thought the walls would crack. "I don't want to talk to you! You call my husband! Call him!"

"Just answer one question…"

I slammed the phone down with all my might before he could finish asking.

The commotion brought my mother-in-law rushing into the room. I was sitting in a chair gasping for breath. "Mom!" I screeched hysterically. "Something's wrong with me! I can't breathe. I feel like someone's choking me."

She said, "Debbie, I think you're having a panic attack."

Although I had never before experienced a true clinical panic attack, I knew she was right. It was the first of countless others to come. They always arrive after a trigger event, something that brings me too close to what happened during that terrible operation. Once they begin I must allow them to run their course. They're like machines that, when switched on, must complete their full cycle.

47

The records and the hospital categorically denied the possibility that I could have been aware during the procedure.... The head of anesthesiology had written that I dreamt it.

I started seeing an MD because I wanted to speak with a medical professional who might have some insight into what was going on inside me. He prescribed Xanax, a tranquilizer, so I could get some sleep. But even when I used it I had to sleep sitting up in a recliner because lying prone would almost inevitably cause vivid flashbacks.

The medication didn't stop my constant nightmares, either. Usually, I'd be undergoing a botched operation in a strange, filthy, dark hospital. I'd be utterly alone and completely helpless. The doctors were more like monsters than people. And the fact that I'd dream of exactly the same procedure again and again made matters even more terrifying. There were other nightmares, too, worse ones. I'd watch people being tortured or be tortured myself and I'd wake up literally screaming. I still have such dreams. They're so bestial I don't like thinking about them.

Much later, my husband and I got the chance to talk with members of the hospital staff and review my records. My symptoms of post-traumatic stress were tearing me and my family apart. The records and the hospital categorically denied the possibility that I could have been aware during the procedure.

One physician told me, "Oh, it must have been something from your past resurfacing."

Another insisted that the drugs I received caused me to hallucinate the entire incident.

The head of anesthesiology had written that I dreamt it. He told my husband, "If your wife *was* in pain, we quickly addressed it." What a lie! I was screaming. But none of them could account for the fact that I knew what was going on during the time I should have been unconscious.

I was unable to go back to work at the hospital for a month. What kept me away was more than feelings of insecurity. I didn't want to run into the anesthesiologist. Just the thought of him brought on violent emotions, and I didn't want to put them to the test in a real encounter. But finally, I believed I had myself under control. Sure enough, it wasn't long before we met. He wanted to sit down and talk privately and I complied. "What happened?" I asked.

"You were dreaming," he answered immediately.

Sure enough, it wasn't long before we met. He wanted to sit down and talk privately and I complied.

"What happened?" I asked.

"You were dreaming," he answered immediately.

I became incensed. "Really! Figure the odds that I'd be dreaming I was having exactly that type of surgery with excruciating pain in my lower left quadrant while the staff was laughing. Pretty damn accurate for a dream!"

He shifted nervously and muttered something.

"We're not poo-pooing it!" I continued. "We're not going to sweep it under the rug. It happened! And I want to know why." But I wasn't just letting off steam. I desperately wanted to know what had gone wrong. I really did want an answer. I never got one, though. To this day the staff denies that any mistakes were made. That makes me feel doubly betrayed.

I was never able to deal with the surgeon again. Whenever he appeared I'd have to leave the area. Then I'd run to a telephone and call my husband, hysterical with fear. Realizing what I was going through, he'd say, "Don't worry, Debbie. He can't hurt you now. He can't touch you."

I desperately wanted to know what had gone wrong. I really did want an answer. I never got one, though. To this day the staff denies that any mistakes were made. That makes me feel doubly betrayed.

My co-workers were also sympathetic. They'd cover for me during those moments and tell me later, "God, I hate what they did to you. How could they put you through that?"

Nine months after the incident, I fell into major depression and then was diagnosed with multiple sclerosis.

I'm truly thankful to God for my husband and the strength of our marriage. Without him I don't think I could have survived.

It's been over a year since the operation. Neither the panic attacks nor the nightmares have lessened. But at least I have some perspective on the situation.

I don't know what life has in store for me now, or how long it will be before I'm gone. I have a lot to deal with.

The happy life I used to live is finished. I confess, I think of suicide once in a while. But I have a strong religious faith, too. My belief supports me through the roughest times. Though I don't understand why this happened to me, I do believe there must be some reason. God always has a reason. I concentrate on that. Perhaps by telling my story, by bringing the truth to light, I can help others who've undergone the same trauma. Other victims should know they're not alone. Or maybe, if people finally open their eyes to the problem, they can put a stop to it altogether.

CHAPTER 4

AFTERMATH
"…nowhere to turn for compassion or solace."

he year was 1878, and the renowned French physiologist, Claude Bernard, had just witnessed a clinical demonstration of the effects of curare, a new drug in the medical arsenal derived from a diabolical South American arrow poison. Nothing like it had ever been seen before in the West, for curare causes complete paralysis without affecting consciousness. Bernard, a seasoned professional who had observed countless surgical procedures and vivisections, was shaken to the core by the experimental procedure. Later, in recounting his own reactions to the event, he would ponder whether there could be a fate more horrible than that of an intelligent being watching

While the experience of "coming to" during surgery is terrifying enough, it does not even begin to circumscribe the full horror that anesthetic awareness carries in its wake.

51

Deep psychological scars often linger on well after the actual events have taken place, devastating careers and relationships and draining all joy from life.

his or her own surgery, and becoming in essence a living corpse.

Few descriptions can better touch the real quality of anesthetic awareness. Ironically, as has been noted earlier, surgeons began using purified forms of curare itself in the 1950s as an adjunct to general anesthesia.[1] While the experience of "coming to" during surgery is terrifying enough, it does not even begin to circumscribe the full horror that anesthetic awareness carries in its wake. For those who have endured such hellish experiences and lived, operating room torment marks only the beginning of a long, difficult road.

Awareness events generate fears and destructive emotions that refuse to stop at the door when the patient leaves the hospital. Deep psychological scars often linger on well after the actual events have taken place, devastating careers and relationships and draining all joy from life. Inner peace is shattered as painful recollections or feelings well up uncontrollably again and again. Anesthetic awareness patients find themselves longing in vain for respite from their enormous burdens of memory. Too often the inordinate range and types of stresses prove too much. Life easily loses its center and meaning for awareness victims in their struggle to cope.

How is life transformed for those who have awakened to find themselves "shut up in a living corpse," and then physically recovered? Does any semblance of normalcy remain?

Studies focusing on the problem all note that awareness patients are extremely reluctant to talk about what happened to them, especially to medical personnel. Commonly, they are overwhelmed by tremendous fears of disbelief, of being considered insane, or of retribution for whistle-blow-ing or trouble making. The agony they endured makes them unwilling to risk any more solely for the sake of making themselves heard.

These misgivings are well founded, because doctors and hospital administrators have been known to dismiss reports of anesthetic awareness out of hand. And if no one is willing to listen, why should one bother to talk?

Physicians have lacked the skills and resources to understand how to listen to and get help for patients who have undergone an awareness experience. Only recently does there appear to be a growing recognition among healthcare professionals that patients must be listened to, the possibility of awareness must be acknowledged, and referrals must be made for counseling assistance. Sadly, there have been many victims of awareness who have had the misfortune of being told after the fact that awareness does not exist or does not represent anything out of the ordinary.

Clinically, the spectrum of psychological problems noted by awareness patients frequently appears following any extraordinarily terrifying event that falls far outside the range of normal human endurance: in this case, lucid consciousness coupled with total paralysis and nightmarish pain. Psychologists simply term the syndrome *post-traumatic stress disorder*, or PTSD, but the four-letter acronym covers a tragic abyss into which many lives have irretrievably plunged.

PTSD is marked by a number of characteristic features including nervousness, suspiciousness, exaggerated response to minor stress, upwelling of unpleasant memories, forgetfulness, emotional flatness, and phobias. It can be acute or chronic, and its onset may be delayed for weeks or even years following the trauma that lies at its source.

Those who have been hit hard by natural disasters, serious accidents, war, violent crime, and torture commonly manifest PTSD. Such "standard" precursors to PTSD, however shocking, generate thought processes that can later be used as safety valves—ways to rationalize and justify what has taken place. In this connection, it is vital to note that no one, even the least informed, doubts the essential, sometimes terrible realities that result from conflicts, social deviance, and flukes of nature. However, the fact of anesthetic awareness is known to only a small fraction of the public. Victims, their families, and their therapists make up virtually the entire group. Anesthetic awareness is just starting to receive public attention, but it commands no political interest or large-scale financial concern.

Tragedies stemming from natural disasters, technological and mechanical failures, and other seemingly unpreventable occurrences have come to be understood as part and parcel of ordinary life, a price we must pay for luxuries like urban development, rapid transit, indoor heating, etc. Humankind has been subject to these sorts of occurrences since the dawn of civilization.

Pain and loss that are the deliberate results of human action are harder to comprehend, but unfortunately are equally prevalent throughout history. War and its awful consequences have been studied and debated since men first took up weapons. Crime has been similarly analyzed. Today's muggers are not all that different from the pirates of old. And torture was as popular during the Inquisition as it is in certain nations today.

But PTSD arising out of anesthetic awareness is something new under the sun—a tragedy without precedence in human history. When patients submit to surgery, they are not being swept away on an adverse natural or political tide. Rather, they are making a deliberate, highly informed decision. They believe they know what their options are and the full array of dangers they face. Even when patients are informed of the possibility of anesthetic awareness by their anesthesia provider during the pre-anesthesia meeting, the amount of information provided is often minimal and superficial at best.

Thus, when a person regains consciousness while under the knife, the shock of realization alone can be equal to or even greater than the sensation of physical agony. Preparation has been shown to be of value in overcoming emotions stirred by traumatic stress. But there really is little preparation for awakening during surgery.

This quality of unexpectedness magnifies the extent of psychological impact beyond anything seen in battlefields, crushed vehicles, or interrogation chambers. Not only is the physical pain overwhelming, the situation itself is impossible to begin with. The mind grapples for some kind of solid conceptual footing but there is none.

The majority of victims are denied the definitive and relatively quick relief of death. They are so surprised that they cannot muster even a mythic framework for the experience. Their personalities rip apart at the seams.

The majority of victims are denied the definitive and relatively quick relief of death. They are so surprised that they cannot muster even a mythic framework for the experience. Their personalities rip apart at the seams. Thus, PTSD induced by consciousness during surgery has a uniquely distressing character. Like a rabid dog, it rages throughout the psyche, immune to reason and insight.

But the extent of this tragedy is augmented yet again. Because anesthetic awareness has received so little attention from the surgical and anesthesia communities, the soul-shattering lack of context that deprives a victim of humanity in the operating room continues uninterrupted when he or she finally attempts to return to a semblance of normal life.

Doctors, nurses, and administrators sometimes deny the reality of the experience itself even when faced with accurate accounts of surgical procedures detailed by patients who were supposedly unconscious. This "professional denial" throws sufferers into a mind-wrenching bind: own up to the experience and be labeled "disturbed" or "troublesome," or attempt to suppress an event so awful it cannot be forgotten.

Together, all these pressures add up to long-term misery. Taken off-guard, catapulted into a situation where helplessness combines with fiendish torment, ignored or belittled by "experts" afterwards, awareness victims are often forced to rely wholly on their own resources. Often, they are not sufficient.

Awareness patients frequently manifest particularly severe and atypical forms of PTSD. Painful recollections and out-of-control emotions are unusually powerful and long-lived. Nightmares, fears, frightening visions and sensory perceptions haunt both waking and sleeping hours.

Typically, paralyzing alienation leads to decreased job performance or loss of ability to work. Sex lives dwindle away as depression intrudes. Ordinary emotional reactions are blunted or distorted. Harmless, everyday situations suddenly assume terrifying aspects.

For example, almost all victims are inordinately afraid of lying down in darkened rooms because the conditions mimic their closed-eyed state on the operating table. So instead of resting normally in their bedrooms, they are reduced to sitting in brightly illuminated rooms until drowsiness overcomes them. Enclosed areas like automobiles and phone booths cannot be tolerated because they approximate the unnatural isolation endured during anesthetic consciousness.

Simple gestures of courtesy and friendliness hark back to the surgeon or anesthesia provider's hollow reassurances and so may be misinterpreted or rebuked. Even minor medical procedures are viewed with alarm and avoided if possible; major ones almost invariably revive the original trauma.

Perhaps the single most characteristic feature of awareness PTSD is involuntary reliving of the causative event. Flashbacks may be completely spontaneous or elicited by circumstances that perceptually or emotionally remind the victims of their experience. These flashbacks tend to be remarkably vivid and convincing; the person may literally believe he or she has been conveyed back to the operating room. Not unsurprisingly, fight-or-flight behavior may occur under such circumstances: The victim first freezes, then suddenly explodes into action, attacking or fleeing.

Radical instinctive reactions of this type have been literally hardwired into our brains. They reflect the animal we evolved from long ago. And throughout the long years of prehistory, they served adaptive purposes quite admirably. But to the awareness victim, these reactions are mindlessly destructive impulses that cut through and destroy all bonds of civilized life and interpersonal relationships. Witnesses to flashback episodes typically do not understand the patient's underlying condition

Awareness PTSD syndromes usually last for years; often they do not abate for a lifetime. Some acquaintances and spouses who cannot fathom the far-reaching personality changes simply drop away.

and are themselves left confused and fearful. Thus, the patient's pain ruthlessly expands into social groups, friends, and family alike.

Awareness PTSD syndromes usually last for years; often they do not abate for a lifetime. Some acquaintances and spouses who cannot fathom the far-reaching personality changes simply drop away. Others turn their own hurt on the sufferer or innocent parties. A vicious circle is thus created, where the victim, perpetually misunderstood and continually denied help or empathy, is progressively turned into a mental cripple, unable to work or love.

Worst of all, perhaps more than any other type of victim in today's society, the anesthetic awareness patient has virtually nowhere to turn for compassion or solace, since awareness is still not fully accepted by the medical community for the terrifying event that it is.

In cases where consciousness is only partially aroused during invasive procedures or where memory does not remain fully intact, even more puzzling psychological symptoms can become manifest. In this category are individuals who were cognizant to a greater or lesser degree of calloused or uncomplimentary remarks made by medical personnel just prior to, during, or after surgery. Physicians, believing the patient is "dead to the world," are known to relieve stress with grim or off-color humor at such times. But when grossly offensive words filter into the anesthetized mind, they convey an incredibly potent emotional charge.

The reason words of this type are so powerful is not difficult to see: Under anesthetic agents, a person's mental condition becomes closely allied with that produced in hypnosis. Individuals in both states are hyper-suggestible; in other words, concepts that would normally be ignored are passed uncensored through the filter of higher brain centers. This is why a normally inhibited hypnotized subject immediately acts upon a suggestion to sing or dance, or a cheerful subject begins weeping when told that the world has come to an end.

Among other things, higher cerebral centers cast a critical eye on verbalized input. They are vital for us to discriminate successfully between the plausible and the ridiculous. When they are partially "turned off" by hypnosis or drugs like anesthetics, the most absurd or insulting comments may easily be accepted as literal fact.

Thus, negative mental changes brought on by disparaging remarks about the patient's appearance, plight, or human worth during an awareness experience can well be imagined. As is the case with hypnotic states, comments frequently cannot be specifically recalled, yet the implied suggestions are absorbed anyway to wreak havoc later.

Research indicates that memories of surgery without explicit recall may be much more common than doctors have traditionally assumed. Studies in this field show a high prevalence of task learning without overt memory, and scientists have repeatedly found that suggestions made during anesthesia are frequently followed postoperatively, although subjects cannot remember being exposed to the suggestions.

When awareness victims do obtain insight into their conditions and deliberately seek help, they have very few places to turn. Experienced and knowledgeable post-traumatic therapists are a rare breed. Because PTSD often produces declining earning capacity, sufferers are rarely able to accommodate heavy fee schedules. Thus, there is little incentive for the ambitious psychiatrist or psychologist to concentrate on post-traumatic stress. The handful of existing specialists all note how awareness patients mistake the grossly abnormal events of their surgery for abnormalities in themselves. Long-term psychological problems can spring forth like weeds.

Recovery can only follow a painful pattern of adjustment that is unique for each victim. The difference between effective and ineffective counseling lies primarily in how the therapist views ongoing problems like re-experiencing, avoidance, sensitivity, and self-blame.

Most mental health professionals will not acknowledge that anesthetic awareness is a genuine objective phenomenon. They are taught to regard symptoms like these not as the natural result of unusual events but as products of inherent personality flaws or neurotic—sometimes even psychotic—defense mechanisms.

As a result, victims are subject to further damage because "helpful intervention" really represents little more than a continuation of physician denial. Coerced into the idea that awareness PTSD originates in their own defects, patients inflict further harm on their already fragile self-images.

The handful of existing specialists all note how awareness patients mistake the grossly abnormal events of their surgery for abnormalities in themselves. Long-term psychological problems can spring forth like weeds.

Although numerous social services exist to help victims of violent crime, war, and natural disaster, until the past few years nothing was available for people traumatized by anesthetic awareness. More is at stake here than pure economics. Therapeutic progress means little unless patients can be socially reintegrated.

Yet, because their problem is never exposed to society at large, awareness patients endure tremendous isolation and loneliness. Bonds of mutual trust and sympathy are difficult or impossible to forge under such trying circumstances. Furthermore, the trauma can never be purged unless the victims feel they can join hands with fellow human beings for common goals.

Anesthetic awareness does not begin and end in the hospital: This is why it is more unpleasant than many care to contemplate. Shock and pain represent just the beginning. Only when awareness victims try to pick up the threads of their lives does the true agony of their situation come into play.

REFERENCE

1. Thatcher VS. *History of Anesthesia With Emphasis on the Nurse Specialist.* Philadelphia, Pa: JB Lippincott; 1953:174-175.

CHAPTER 5

LOOKING OUT THE WINDOW

"I flash back with every breath I take."

s I sat looking out the window on a cold winter afternoon 15 months after my surgery, my mind drifted to the coldness I felt lying helpless on the operating table. Frozen in time, frozen in pain and fear, alone. All alone.

More than a year later I was still alone, locked inside a body that no longer functioned as it had before. I was no longer myself, and was still desperately trying to understand what had happened to me in that OR.

Why had I been awake? How could this have happened to me? I was strong. I was healthy. I had a positive attitude and unbreakable spirit. And yet, when I was lying there through that surgery, I was nothing. I was nobody.

Why had I been awake? How could this have happened to me? I

61

was strong. I was healthy. I had a positive attitude and unbreakable spirit. And yet, when I was lying there through that surgery, I was nothing. I was nobody. I couldn't move, couldn't speak, couldn't even take a breath! It was a feeling of suffocation, and of dying.

I remembered the terror of thinking, "I'm going to die alone and no one will even know that I was awake when I died. No one will even know the fear that is running through my body."

I sat there looking out the window, sensing the coldness outside and actually feeling it on the windowpane as my hand touched it. I flashed back, seemingly with every breath, to that operating room. I felt so helpless, even as I sat in that chair 15 months later. When was this going to stop? When was this nightmare going to end? When were all the screams, no longer silent, going to end?

At times, in the middle of the night, I dreamt of being trapped back on the table, the smell of my flesh burning, wanting to gag.

Each and everyday was so long, trying to figure out how to put my life back together. I'd say to myself, "You have to, Jeanette. You're a survivor. You can do this!"

Then I'd be off again, panicked with fear. The Jeanette I knew, the Jeanette I was, was gone. Every day was a struggle. Every morning I'd wake up thinking it's going to be over and come to find out it was not over. Some days were even worse.

Every day was a struggle to read, to write, to get the terrible thoughts out of my head. I knew how to do things, but I just couldn't do them. The actions got blocked or lost in my mind. All the things I took for granted, were gone. They were in me but I couldn't bring them out. I could think things but I couldn't say them. I could spell, but I couldn't write. When was the nightmare going to end? Was the nightmare ever going to be over? I wondered if maybe I was dead. Maybe it was all a dream, an illusion.

The snow started to fall as I looked out the window. It was so beautiful. I used to love winter. I used to love playing in the snow, skiing, building snowmen, and sledding with my daughters. Now the winter was no longer enjoyable. The heat was turned up to 85 degrees in the house. I wore a robe, sweater, and warm socks, and wrapped myself in a blanket and afghan because I couldn't stand the cold anymore. I couldn't smell the cold air—it hurt my nose, my throat, and made me shiver. It was not only from the coldness, but from the memories that lurked within the coldness. I had to find out what happened, what went wrong. I knew it wasn't my fault. I knew I had nothing to do with it. "There must be someone out there who can help me," I thought. "I will continue to look, continue to search, and I will always continue to pray because God only knows how much I want to get back to me and how much I want my life to be my own again." Then my mind would spin: "There's nowhere to go, no one to talk to, no one who understands. I can't even talk to my anesthesiologist or the surgeon. They don't want to deal with it. They don't want to acknowledge it!" It was not a matter of money or suing—not for me anyway. It was a matter of a higher price—my life. I wanted my life back as I knew it, as I had lived it, as I had accepted it. *My* life.

I looked in the mirror and I looked the same. I spoke the same, I even tried to act the same and hide the phobias that overwhelmed me from

"There's nowhere to go, no one to talk to, no one who understands. I can't even talk to my anesthesiologist or the surgeon. They don't want to deal with it. They don't want to acknowledge it!" It was not a matter of money or suing—not for me anyway. It was a matter of a higher price—my life.

63

hour to hour. But inside I didn't know where I went. I even thought about going back to that operating room because maybe, as ludicrous as it sounded, if I walked back into that operating room whatever I lost of myself in there might return to me. But I couldn't even get close to a hospital or a doctor, let alone the smell of an operating room and that feeling of coldness that awaited me.

So what could I do? Where could I go? How could I fix me? I prayed to God over and over to help me. I yelled and screamed in frustration to God to stop it, change it, heal me, release me. I begged God to release me from the nightmares and the gripping cold they brought.

I knew that God never gives us more than we can handle. So was this a test? I asked, "Are you testing me, Lord, to see how strong I really am?" But is it necessary to test any human being like that? For what purpose? Would it have been easier to be weak? But I was strong. If I had been weak, I would have died. And then would it have been over? Or would it have continued on? What was this about? What was the difference between life and death? Was there any? All I knew for sure was that my life had turned dim and cold.

I thought, "I must be living in Hell...."

Each and everyday was a struggle to stay alive as I once knew life—a struggle to be positive, loving, caring, giving, kind, and patient. And at times I couldn't even stand myself. I couldn't stand the crying anymore. I couldn't stand feeling scared, like a little girl.

I was tired of being embarrassed. At one point, I was at the grocery store standing in line, and everything was fine for a short while. Then all of a sudden there it was—that wretched smell of my flesh burning as I was being cut and cauterized. Where did it come from? From inside my head, where it was locked in my subconscious. The smell got stronger and stronger. My mouth began to water. And I was going to throw up.

64

I pleaded, "Please God, don't let me throw up. Please don't embarrass me like this."

The next thing I remember, I was begging the check-out girl for a bag. Then I quickly leaned over the register to grab a bag because the girl had no idea what was happening. I knelt down on the floor and threw up. No one saw me except for the people who were behind me. How embarrassing.

Standing up, I apologized to everyone and said, "I'm sorry, I haven't been feeling well. Sorry." No one knew what to say, because there wasn't anything they could say.

"Why God, why?" I pleaded. "It would have been easier if I had died on that damned table than to go through this. When is it going to stop?"

I paid for the groceries and got out of there as fast as I could. I threw my things in the car and sat there crying like a 2-year-old whose toy had just broken.

I was not only physically and visually upset, but I had to figure out how to get out of the parking lot.

I tried to remember, "Where is my street? How do I get home?"

I thought maybe I could call somebody. I got out of the car, tried to catch my breath, walked around the car a few times, got back in the car, and grabbed my cell phone.

Then, I frantically asked myself, "What is the number?"

I couldn't think of the number! So I started pushing numbers and got somebody, anybody, except whoever I was looking for to come and help me. I hung up.

"Why God, why?" I pleaded. "It would have been easier if I had died on that damned table than to go through this. When is it going to stop? You have to stop it God. You have to take this from me. You have to free me.

"Someone out there, help me. I'm desperate. I can't take it anymore. I'm tired."

Please Lord, I'll do whatever you want. Help me, sweet Jesus. Where are you? I'm lost down here. I can't find my way home. Help me. Someone out there, help me. I'm desperate. I can't take it anymore. I'm tired."

I could feel myself slowly sinking down into my soul. I wanted to curl up, close my eyes and pray that not another whoosh of air in anyway would pass through my body so that I could be released from this pain.

It didn't happen. No one answered. I was still sitting in my car. I was still at the grocery store. I would try to find my way home. So I backed up and started driving.

Thank God, some things started to look familiar. I was so thankful and told myself over and over again, "Okay, this is the right way. Okay, Jeanette, good. Keep going. Everything's all right. Stay calm. Just stay calm. Think. Just think and stay calm."

And then I saw my street, and finally my house. A sense of relief washed over me.

I got out of the car and went in the house. I sat on the sofa, on the chairs, and on the floors. I wound up sitting on the steps, crying. I cried so hard I thought I was going to throw up again.

By then it was almost time for Lisa and Valerie to come home from school. I had to make sure everything was all right, at least outwardly. I didn't want them to know my pain, my fear, my worries, or my concerns. So I began to make dinner and pretend it was business as usual. Soon my girls would be home. Since the surgery, I had lived in panic and fear every second they were gone. I looked at my watch, then at the clock, and cautioned myself that soon they'd be home.

I told myself not to panic this time, because I had learned over the past 15 months that if they were five or 10 minutes late, it was okay. I knew that if they were a little late it didn't mean something had happened to them.

I also realized that here I was, a grown woman, and I was scared to be by myself.

I focused on the fact that soon my girls would be home. There was no one in this world I trusted more than my girls. No one in this world could love me more than they did. And sure enough, they came through the door and I rushed to them. I hugged them and kissed them and told them how much I loved them.

As they looked at me—confused, worried, concerned, and whatever else they felt—they assured me by saying, "That's okay, Momma, we're home."

By now, they knew this as my everyday routine.

So often I prayed, "God, just please let them have fun at school and learn. Don't let them worry about me all through the day. Let them know that it's okay. Give me the strength not to show them my own fears. Help me God, and help them. Help them God, to help me."

Then came dinnertime. It was almost normal. We talked and laughed. We teased each other. I cleaned up after dinner, and made sure the girls did their homework, took their baths. I laid out their clothes for the next day and made sure that everything was in their book bags.

This routine was very important because in the mornings I was so exhausted from not sleeping all night that if I didn't take care of things in the evening I'd forget something, and then I might get a call from the school to bring it to them. Sometimes I could make that drive, and sometimes I couldn't find my way there. Then I would feel terrible guilt. My girls were my life. So needless to say, I made sure that everything was taken care of before bedtime.

I kept telling myself and them, "Everything will be okay. It's going to get better. It will be better tomorrow." But as I would say or think that, I didn't really know if I believed it.

As the girls got ready for bed, I fixed myself a cup of tea. It was colder out now, and I would turn up the heat, but still I couldn't get warm. It was dark, and I needed more lights on. I realized that the house must have looked like a Christmas tree from the outside because I had so many lights on. The only lights that weren't on were my children's bedroom lights.

I drifted off to sleep, only to abruptly awaken a short while later, gasping for air because I couldn't breathe. Crying and shaking from fear, I had had the nightmare of dying on that table…dying alone. The pain ran through every fiber of my body. Every ounce of my being was in pain and screaming. It was captured and trapped inside of me.

Once again my body couldn't move, couldn't breathe, couldn't speak, couldn't even shed a tear. In my mind I was screaming and crying, begging and pleading, but there was nothing. There was no one.

I felt the humiliation all over again. I remembered what it was like to scream, "My God, my God, why have you forsaken me? Help me God. I don't want to leave my children! I don't want to die yet! Don't leave me. Don't deny me. Don't punish me. Take the suffering away. Help me God."

And then in my mind, the next slice of the scalpel ripped more of my flesh. My insides were laid open, and I felt like a zipper down my body had been pulled apart. Slowly I began to realize where I was—that it was all the nightmare. "It's okay," I told myself. "I'm not in the hospital, I'm not on the operating table, I'm not dying. I'm home, I'm home, I'm home. It's okay. Everything's all right. Just breathe. Just breathe, it's okay. Look around. See, I'm home. Oh my God, how much more can I take?"

I felt so tortured and alone. Nobody knew what to do for me or how to help me. I was not the only one going through this, I was putting my family through hell. I needed to know why this had happened to me, and to understand what it was all about. I needed to find some kind of explanation.

The next day I looked in the phone book to see who I could find. There had to be someone out there who could understand what had happened to me, who could help me put all the pieces of the puzzle together so I could get on with my life.

I looked in the psychology/psychiatry section. I was trying to find the closest person to where I lived, because it didn't matter how good the doctor was, as long as the drive wasn't far. I most likely would not have been able to find the office, and if I did, I wouldn't have been able to get back home.

One phone call after another I asked, "Have you dealt with someone who was awake through their surgery?"

"No, but you can come in and we can talk about it," was the usual reply.

"Well, if you haven't dealt with anyone previously, how are you going to help me?" It didn't make sense. I'd hang up and try another number.

"Have you ever dealt with someone who was awake during surgery and remembers all the details?"

"No, but if you come in, we can talk about it."

I felt so tortured and alone. Nobody knew what to do for me or how to help me. I was not the only one going through this, I was putting my family through hell.

One phone call after another I asked, "Have you dealt with someone who was awake through their surgery?"

"No, but you can come in and we can talk about it," was the usual reply.

> *"...I'm willing to help you find the answers you need."*
>
> *That was all I needed to hear. I booked the appointment for that afternoon. I was so happy and excited—finally someone was willing to help me!*

More numbers. After about the 30th call, I said, "The hell with it." I decided to look for someone who was close to my home. The doctor seemed very sympathetic on the phone.

"No, I have never heard of anyone being awake, but I believe that you were, and I have worked with people who have experienced similar things," she told me. "Their experiences were not exactly like yours, but it sounds like your pain is similar to theirs. And although I've never worked with someone who's been awake through surgery, I'm willing to help you find the answers you need."

That was all I needed to hear. I booked the appointment for that afternoon. I was so happy and excited—finally someone was willing to help me!

I got in my car and thanked God that the doctor was only a street away. As I drove around the block, I was so excited. I finally felt a sense of hope for the first time in a long time.

I pulled into the parking lot and quickly prayed, "Heavenly father, I beg you to please be here for me. Help this person help me. Help *me*, God. I need my life back. I'm at the end of my rope. If I can't find someone to help me, I'm lost forever. I can't live that way. Please understand. I'm begging you now to help me. Amen."

I got out of my car and walked in. So many chairs in the waiting room. A woman came out and I wondered if it was the doctor I'd talked with on the phone. It wasn't. It was a different therapist, and she reassured me that my therapist would be with me soon.

I nervously picked up a magazine and began to read. I tried to keep my mind occupied so I wouldn't get scared. The last thing I wanted was to meet this person and go into a panic attack. I was pretty good at that. I did it nearly every day ... sometimes a couple times a day.

So as I began to read the magazine, I looked around, hoping that soon she would walk out and ask me to come in.

Finally, the door opened and a client left. The therapist looked at me, smiling, and asked, "Are you Jeanette?"

"Yes, I am."

"Please, come in," she said.

I got up nervously, keeping a positive attitude and thinking to myself, "God, please, please let her help me. Let her help me, God. This has to work." She looked at me and asked me to fill out some paperwork. "So what else is new?" I thought.

After completing the form, I handed it back to her and she began to read it. I saw the expression on her face, knowing that her reaction would tell me the truth. She had never dealt with someone like me before.

She quietly put my paperwork in a folder, then looked at me very seriously and said, "I'm sorry. I'm sorry you had to go through such a horrible ordeal. Do you want to tell me more about it?"

Of course I did. I had been waiting for so long. I had been waiting almost a year and a half to talk about it with somebody who could possibly help me. My family was tired of hearing about it. My friends were tired of hearing about it. But I had to talk about it. Did I want to talk about it? Of course I wanted to talk about it! I wanted to tell her everything.

And so we began. I recalled the nightmare once again. And before I knew it, my 50-minute session was up. Yet there was so much more to say!

I begged, "Can I tell you one more thing? I need to tell you something. Every night when I go to bed, I dream of being frozen back on that operating table. I feel the surgeon cutting me open, smell my flesh burning, feel the pain in my chest and down my left arm and in my neck and on the left side of my face. I hear ringing in my head that's so loud it shuts out my screams. But they don't hear. They don't care. They don't even know. And tonight when I go to bed, what do I do? How can I help myself? How can I sleep one night, even if it's just for a couple of hours. I'm so tired. I want to sleep. I want to rest. What do I do?"

I looked in her face, and could tell she didn't know what to tell me. So she asked me a question: "What do you think would help you?" My frustration returned. If I knew, I wouldn't be asking, I'd be doing it; if I knew, I would be sleeping at night. I had tried everything I knew of. Nothing seemed to work.

I earnestly said, "I was hoping you could tell me something. I will try anything. I'll do anything. I trust you. I haven't trusted anybody for 15 months. But for whatever reason, I trust you."

She looked at me, searching carefully for the right words to pass along to me. Softly, gently, and calmly she said to me, "Jeanette, I'm learning about this with you. This is the first time I've ever heard of this happening, but I believe you. I believe you were awake. I'm going to talk to someone—a friend of mine who works in anesthesia. I'm going to ask her some questions to see if she can help me with you."

My confidence in her rose, and also my confidence in myself. I knew she was telling me the truth and that she was not trying to dodge anything.

She said simply, "So when you ask me what to do tonight, how you should sleep, I don't know yet. But soon, between the two of us, we'll be able to figure this out, and we'll be able to change it. Trust that." I had to. That was where my road ended.

I left and got into my car. I had drawn a map from my house around the block to make sure I could get home. I made it. Now I was both trembling and crying again.

Another night. Another nightmare. Another day. It had only been 24 hours since I had seen her, and the realization set in that I would have to live with another week of torment before my next appointment. I *had* to hold on. Every day became more of a challenge. Every night the same.

The following week finally came, and with it my appointment. I couldn't wait to talk with the doctor again. Even though I was paying her just to sit and listen to me, I believed that she really cared and wanted to help. The session began.

"How has this week been?"

Like all the rest—hellish. All of the sudden, my anger came out and the tears started flowing. I couldn't catch my breath, I was crying so hard.

"Tell me what to do, how do I fix this? What am I going to do?" I pleaded.

She said she wanted me to talk to a group of people who would possibly provide me with some support. I agreed. She placed a phone call on my behalf while I waited.

"There's a group meeting tomorrow. Can you make it?" she asked me.

"Of course. I'll be there." I didn't even know what the group was about. I was so desperate for help, I'd have done anything, taken anything, gone anywhere.

"There's a group meeting tomorrow. Can you make it?" she asked me.

"Of course. I'll be there." I didn't even know what the group was about. I was so desperate for help, I'd have done anything, taken anything, gone anywhere.

That night the dreams were more intense. The emotional release in therapy seemed to be causing the dreams to be even deeper, longer, more intense. My body was tighter waking up. There were times in my dreams when I even knew I was dreaming and tried to make myself wake up, but I couldn't. It was like being in two places at once.

I decided to just stay awake. There was no reason to go back to sleep after the nightmare, because I would just end up back where I was. I got the day started: Made breakfast for the girls, made sure they had everything for school, then off they went. Suddenly I was so alone and exhausted I wanted desperately to sleep, but I couldn't.

There were things to be done. Life had to go on. Somehow I found strength to continue. Watching the clock, hour after hour, waiting for the time when the almighty group would be meeting. They had a new member today. They would not be prepared for what I had to tell them, that was for sure. I had asked the therapist if anyone else there had experienced anesthetic awareness, and she'd replied no.

I wondered why I was even going. But I was desperate, and had no choice but to trust her.

At the meeting, the first thing I realized was that I was the only woman there. I was stunned. The therapist began, "Let's all introduce ourselves. We have a new member today. Jeanette is joining us for the first time, as you know. So let's go around and why don't you introduce yourself and explain why you're here. I think that may help her."

"Okay," I thought to myself. "I'm becoming extremely nervous and anxious now." I said a prayer, asking God to protect me from another panic attack and the embarrassment it would bring.

The first man stated his name and his problem. The second, third, fourth, fifth, sixth, seventh, and eighth men followed suit, and it finally

74

dawned on me they were all here with the same problem: They had all been prisoners of war. They all had recurring nightmares. They were all scared. Then the therapist asked me to explain a little bit about my experience. "I don't know why I'm here," I said. "I haven't been to a war like these men. I haven't been captured and held prisoner."

"Pain is pain. Torture is torture. It's all the same. It doesn't matter how you got there. The experience is the same."

"I believe you have," the therapist said. "I believe you have your own war, your own hell, your own nightmares, fears, phobias, and flashbacks. Do you know what the difference is, Jeanette, between you and all these men?"

I thought to myself, "Thank God he realizes that there is a difference." Then I said bluntly, "You were in a war. You were captured. You were tortured."

One of the POWs responded: "Yeah, and so were you. There is no difference. Pain is pain. Torture is torture. It's all the same. It doesn't matter how you got there. The experience is the same."

I stared at him, then started shaking and crying uncontrollably. The two men on either side of me put their hands on my shoulders. "It's okay, Jeanette, let it go. It's okay, tell us about it." They understood! They wanted to listen!

"Do you know what the bitch of it is?" I finally said. "I don't get a medal for it. Nobody cares. I'm still lost, trying to get back. Help me. Somebody please help me."

Everyone got off their chairs and formed a circle around me—some kneeling, some sitting, some standing. Every hand was on me. Men were crying, reassuring me it was going to be okay.

They told me, "We're going to help you get through this. You're not alone. Never again will you be alone. Let us help. Open up and let us in."

They had no idea what they were asking! I didn't even know where the door was to my mind, to my soul, to my life! I didn't know where the door was to let anyone in or anything out. But that was okay with them. They understood. Everyone gave me a suggestion on what to do about the nightmares. Good suggestions. The most important advice I received was not to lay down. Don't lay flat on your back, they told me, otherwise you'll flash back faster. After that, the five pillows I'd been propping myself up with turned into 10 pillows. I was virtually sitting straight up in bed.

Cut back on the caffeine, they told me. Avoid alcohol. Don't take any pills to sleep. They lock you in. Don't take any drugs. I thought, "That's the last thing I need!" It definitely was the last thing I wanted. Even in the hospital I refused medication. I didn't trust anyone to give me anything. Drugs were supposed to keep me unconscious during the surgery and that didn't happen, so how could I expect them to help me now?

The group session was a blessing. I was beginning to find trust again. I trusted these men, and I trusted my therapist. For so long I hadn't trusted anyone or anything except my children. I would look at their young, beautiful, precious faces as they innocently tried to support me and comfort me, and wonder how I could ever pay them back. They had no idea that they were saving their mother's life! When I woke up in the middle of the night, Lisa would hear me and run to my bed, climb in, and hold me in her arms.

"It's okay, Momma. It's okay," she'd say. "It's just a dream. It's just a dream, Momma. It's over. You're here. You're here with Lisa and Valerie and you're safe and we love you so much, Momma. It's okay, do you believe me?"

How difficult it is to look into your child's eyes when she is so desperately trying to save you, out of her own fear of losing you, and out of pure, innocent love!

"Of course I believe you, Lisa," I'd tell her. "I trust you with my life. Even though right now it's upside down, I trust you with it. Hopefully, I'll get it back together. I'm trying real hard, Lisa. I promise. I swear to God, Lisa, I'm trying. I'm so sorry you have to go through this. So sorry I woke you up crying in my sleep. I had the dream again, where they were hurting me."

And then the guilt set in for even sharing this hellish nightmare with my child. What would it do to her? What fears would she have? What scars? "God help her if she has to go into a hospital," I would think. "She or Valerie. After what happened to me; seeing what I'm going through. What would it do to them?"

I learned what the body can endure and tolerate for two hours and 47 minutes—the length of time my surgery lasted. I really didn't think I was going to live.

During those times, I would force myself to stop. I'd swallow hard and get angry, pushing my emotions deep down inside me. I pretended like I was going to sleep in my child's arms until I could hear her breathing and knew she was asleep. But I wouldn't fall asleep myself —I just didn't let her know.

Time stretched on—another day, another night, another week, another month. And then I realized it wasn't even the days, the weeks, and months—it was the minutes and hours that seemed to stretch on forever and never end. It's amazing how long 24 hours can seem. I learned what the body can endure and tolerate for two hours and 47 minutes—the length of time my surgery lasted. I really didn't think I was going to live. I really didn't think anyone was going to understand. While I was on that operating table, my faith was put to a terrible test—my faith in medicine, and my faith in God.

After two hours and 47 minutes of living hell, I had to ask, "Where were you, God?"

And when I asked that question, the first thing that came into my head was that he must have trusted me. God must have trusted me to bear this burden. It didn't make sense at the time, but I supposed—hoped—that eventually it would. My faith had been tested, but remained strong. Although I had my doubts, I believed God was with me, even on that operating table. No one suffers in vain. I kept praying even when I didn't want to. I kept trusting. It helped me to not feel so alone. I just needed to know that there was a reason for what happened. My breakthrough moment came during another visit to my therapist.

I couldn't wait to talk with her again. Sometimes my anger was so strong I just didn't know where to put it. Such anger runs counter to my nature—I am not an angry person. At least, I hadn't been. I kept asking what I thought were reasonable questions, but I wasn't getting any reasonable explanations. So I kept searching: What else could I do? Give up? Lay down and die? If I was supposed to die, I had had my opportunity in the operating room.

I was sitting in my therapist's office again. I always came early. Another patient left the office, a friend by face only. As I took my seat I wondered what the other person was there for—thinking, ridiculously, it could not possibly be as severe as my own situation. But in reality, it's all the same, only the circumstances change. Pain is pain. Fear is fear.

My therapist looked at me. "I'm not going to ask you how you're doing this week because you got upset with me last week when I asked you that question," she said. "I guess by now I should know how you're doing. So do you want to talk about what this past week has been like? Any changes? Anything different? Or do you just want to sit here and not say a word?"

And you know what? That sounded pretty good to me. So that's exactly what I did. I just sat there, not speaking a word. I listened to the clock—every second that ticked by for 50 minutes. My therapist didn't say a word either. She didn't even look at me. I would glance at her now and then to see if she was and I'd look away. Actually, for the first time in a long time, I felt peaceful.

She finally pointed out to me that my time was up. But before I left, she wanted to give me something. She told me she had spoken to a friend of hers in anesthesia. My eyes widened.

She held a paper in her hand and said, "I have something for you that proves what I have said all along. You're not crazy. You didn't dream this. You're not making it up. It happened to you. It's real. And you're not alone."

She held a paper in her hand and said, "I have something for you that proves what I have said all along. You're not crazy. You didn't dream this. You're not making it up. It happened to you. It's real. And you're not alone."

It was the third happiest day of my life—behind the two days when I gave birth to my children. She handed me a piece of paper. It was a publication about awareness under anesthesia. I was shocked and started shaking terribly. I began to cry. It was real, it had happened to me! I didn't realize until then that even I had begun to question whether my experience was real. I couldn't read the publication right then, so I asked if I could take it home.

She said, "Of course. It's yours. Take it home and we'll talk about it next week. But if you need me before then, you know I'm always here for you. Call me, no matter what time it is."

That was all I needed to hear. I had something concrete in my hands to show the world what nobody understood and I had somebody that was going to be there for me, to help me and support me through this. I was no longer alone. I was no longer alone intellectually, and I was no longer alone psychologically. I couldn't drive home fast enough. I got in the house, sat down on the sofa, and began to read this piece of paper that became my lifeline, my survival, my understanding, my everything. I was holding everything in my hands and it was only a piece of paper.

I began to read it. It spoke of people being awake during surgery—feeling the pain, hearing the conversations, feeling helpless—everything that I had said.

It was as if this person knew me inside and out, knew exactly what had happened to me and wrote a paper on it. He was talking about me. I looked at the bottom and saw the name of the person who wrote the article—John Hess. He was in _____. I had to find him. I had to talk to him. He was the key to open my door of survival, of healing, of hope. It was too late to call. I decided to call first thing in the morning. I didn't know how I'd find him, I only knew I had to.

I remember vividly: It was 7 o'clock on a Thursday morning when I called Information. "I need a phone number for John Hess in _____."
No luck. But I didn't give up. I tried again.

"Hold for the number, please." Oh my God, he's real, I thought. This was really going to happen. He was going to help me put my life back together. He would help me home.

My hands trembled as I dialed the number. My heart pounded so hard I could feel it in the back of my throat. I thought my head was going to explode. I was so nervous. Then he answered, "Hello?"

"Hi, my name is Jeanette. I know that you don't know me but I'm hoping and praying to God that you can help me. You see, I had surgery and I was awake and I felt them cutting me. I could feel every slice of the scalpel, I could smell my flesh burning, I tasted the blood spilling down the back of my throat because a tube was cutting me, I felt like I was going to throw up, I don't know what to do! Can you help me? Please, please, don't

80

think that I'm crazy. Please, I'm telling you the truth. What do I do?"

"Well, first of all, you're not crazy," he said. "Second, it did happen and it happens often."

"What do you mean it happens often? I thought I was the only one."

"No, you're not," he said.

"How many times has this happened?"

"Thousands."

"Thousands? How can that be? How can it happen so often yet nobody I talked to knew anything about it?" We talked for awhile, then I asked Mr. Hess about a notice for a symposium in Atlanta at Emory University, which was included in the paper my therapist had given me. A Dr. Peter Sebel was listed as a speaker.

I asked Mr. Hess, "Do you think I should call him? Do you have his phone number? Or can I give you my number and have you ask him to call me? Please, I'm trying to put my life back together, and nobody can help me because nobody knows what I'm talking about. Please don't hang up. I beg you. You're all I've got."

I heard him swallow. I imagined a lump in his throat as he swallowed. He reassured me he wasn't going anywhere and that he would help me. He told me there were many articles written about awareness and that I could read more about it if there was a medical library or university nearby.

"But what about the symposium, do you think I could go?" I asked. "I just want to go to hear other people talk about it."

"Well, first of all, you're not crazy," he said. "Second, it did happen and it happens often."

"What do you mean it happens often? I thought I was the only one."

"No, you're not," he said.

"How many times has this happened?"

"Thousands."

81

"I don't know if you can or not," he replied. "It's for anesthesiologists. I'm a nurse anesthetist."

A nurse anesthetist? I asked him what a nurse anesthetist was. He said he administered anesthesia and stayed with patients throughout their surgeries. He explained that an anesthesiologist was an MD, a doctor who specialized in anesthesia, and he was a registered nurse specializing in anesthesia. He told me to call Atlanta and try to get into the symposium, and that I could call him if I needed him. He wished me luck.

Immediately after I got off the phone with John Hess, I called information for the number of Emory University. Again I began to tremble as I waited for the number. Endless streams of tears ran down my face. When I had the number, I immediately called Emory.

I heard a voice on the other end, "May I help you, please?"

"Yes, I was wondering if I could get a number for Dr. Peter Sebel. I understand he has a symposium coming up on awareness and I would like to come if I may."

The woman asked in a Scottish accent, "Are you an anesthesiologist?"

"No, I'm not. I'm not an anesthesiologist, I'm not a nurse anesthetist, I'm nobody. I was awake during my surgery."

"I'm sorry," she replied. "This is a symposium for anesthesiologists."

"Please, just listen to what I have to say." And as I began to tell my story to the lady, she apologized for me having to go through that. She was sympathetic and full of emotions. For whatever reason, I felt this woman understood what I'd been talking about. I knew in my heart she would help me. Her name was Kathleen.

She told me she needed to talk to Dr. Sebel. She would ask him if I could attend the symposium and get back to me as soon as possible. I thanked her and hung up, wondering if it would ever happen. Again, I still had trouble trusting anyone or anything. How could I not?

That night was extremely difficult. I probably cried for about 12 hours. One nightmare after another. Again, the walls, my entire room—everything was red. My heart pounded in my mouth. I was drenched, my nightgown sticking to my body. I was alone again with nowhere to go, and nobody to talk to at 4 o'clock in the morning! I'm sure John Hess meant well when he said I could call him, but I'm sure he didn't mean at 4 in the morning. So I sat there holding myself together as tight as I possibly could.

A few days passed. No phone calls. I was sure they thought I was crazy. At least I still had that piece of paper that proved what happened to me was real.

A few days passed. No phone calls. I was sure they thought I was crazy. At least I still had that piece of paper that proved what happened to me was real. It was better than nothing.

But since it was true, why wouldn't anyone help me? It all became so confusing again. I was still searching, but getting no answers.

A couple more days passed and I couldn't take it anymore. So I called back to Emory. Kathleen answered the phone again.

"Hi, remember me? I'm the lady who had awareness. I called for Dr. Sebel."

"Oh, well he was out of town. He'll be back tomorrow. I'm sure when he gets back that he will definitely call you," she said.

"Please. Tell him I'm begging him to call me back."

Then I began to cry. I heard the woman's voice softly cracking itself. She understood my pain, I thought. She reassured me that the doctor would call me.

The next day came and I anxiously waited for Dr. Sebel's phone call. Every time the phone rang, I prayed that it was him. Finally, I picked up the phone and there was a man with a British accent on the other end. "Hello, this is Dr. Peter Sebel, can I help you?"

"Yes, Dr. Sebel. I was awake," I blurted out. "I want to come to the symposium. Please let me come to the symposium. I'm begging you, sir. Let me come to the symposium. I just want to learn how to help myself— what to do, what this all means. I need to put my life back together again. I need you to help me. There's nowhere else for me to turn. I'm in counseling but my counselor doesn't understand. I'm trying to explain it to her. I'm hoping she can help me to figure this out. I just want to come and learn. Do you think you can help me? I'll sit in the back and won't say a word. Nobody even has to know what I'm there for. Please."

Dr. Sebel said he was in the middle of surgery and that he would get back to me. An hour passed and no word. I thought they might think I was crazy, but I couldn't help it. I called back. I had to get an answer. I couldn't give up now. I was going to have my life back!

I talked to Kathleen again. She told me that Dr. Sebel gave me permission to join them at the symposium. I couldn't believe it! It was a dream come true! Finally, I was going to figure out what had happened. Maybe I would learn something that would be able to help the rest of the POWs. Maybe I could find a way to cure all of our nightmares and phobias.

CHAPTER 6

SYMPOSIUM
"A miracle…to go."

ow that I had permission to attend the symposium, I needed a ticket to Atlanta and a place to stay. I called the airlines to find out how much a round-trip ticket would cost from Washington, D.C. to Atlanta. The agent responded, "That will be $578. Would you like me to hold a seat for you?" I wondered where I was going to get that kind of money.

"Yes, hold it for me," I said. The agent told me that they could hold the seat for 24 hours. I had a lot of work to do if I was going to come up with $578 that fast. I began to look for something to sell. Fortunately I lived in Virginia, where there must be 10,000 antique stores.

I had an old mirror from my grandmother that I really did not want to give up, but it was the only way I could think of to get the money for Atlanta. So I jumped in my car and took the mirror down to Old Town in Alexandria. I went from store to store asking what I could get for the old mirror, and was told it was worth only about $375.

I just had to find someone to buy the mirror, because I *had* to get to Atlanta to find out what had happened to me in that operating room. I was certain the answers were there. But at this point, Atlanta seemed halfway around the world.

At the end of Old Town on a side street, I saw one last store and decided to take a chance. Up the stairs to the store I went, and with each step I asked God to please help me.

Inside the store, a woman with pitch black hair and blue eyes came from behind the counter to greet me. She asked, "Are you looking for something in particular today?"

"Yes, a miracle," I said.

"What kind of miracle?" asked the woman.

"Well, actually I would like to sell this mirror. I need the money for a plane ticket to go to a meeting," I heard myself saying.

She looked at me and said, "I'm sure you have a reason for doing so."

I told her my story about awareness and at the end she asked me how much my plane ticket cost.

I said, "It's $578. I know this is not worth it but the trip is priceless."

She smiled at me and said, "Let me write you a check."

As she handed me the check, I noticed the total was for $600. I told her that it was more than I needed and she smiled again, put her arm around me and said, "You'll need something to eat until you get there."

Needless to say, I was very grateful. I was also on my way to Atlanta!

I packed and unpacked, and packed again. I pulled together all of my medical records, x-rays, and everything I could think of that might be helpful.

I said to myself, "I'm really going. It's really happening."

I could barely sleep a wink that night but it was okay because I was used to not sleeping anyway. I prayed for hours off and on. I asked God to help me so that I could help others. I asked God to give me the right words to speak when I met Dr. Sebel. More than anything else, I asked for courage.

Finally I drifted off to sleep and then heard the alarm go off. Jumping out of bed and almost falling, I ran to the shower, got dressed and double-checked to make sure that I had everything to take to the airport.

As I sat on the plane, all I could think of was that I was close to God, high up there, and that everything was going to be all right.

Once I landed in Atlanta, I got a cab to the hotel where the symposium was being held. I walked in and froze in my steps when I saw a large room filled with people. I thought to myself, "Oh my God, there are hundreds!"

I walked up to a table where people were checking in and heard a Scottish accent coming from one of the women at the table. I looked at her name badge and saw, "Kathleen." It was her—the lady I had gotten permission from to attend the symposium.

I walked up to her and said, "I'm Jeanette."

She smiled and shook my hand. I asked if Dr. Sebel was there yet and she pointed to a man with a beard and glasses. I thanked her and went up to Dr. Sebel to introduce myself.

He looked at me cautiously as if to make sure I wasn't crazy. Then he smiled and I took a deep breath to relax. I gave him a pack of papers with all of the information that I had about my awareness. He told me he was busy and had to run, but that he would see me at the symposium.

I went up to my room and will always remember how alone I felt. I was the only person there who had experienced awareness. I wondered if anyone knew who I was? How could they? They had never met me before. Probably no one even knew I was even there. Why would they? I felt like a big secret. Why not? Dr. Sebel did not know me or even if my story of awareness was true at that point. After all, we had never met until that day.

I laid down on the bed and was overwhelmed with fear as the tears flooded my pillow. I suddenly wanted to get out of there. The fear became stronger as I wondered how I would be treated by everyone. Would they blame me for what happened, or even worse, would they wonder why I was even there?

Well, like it or not, I was there, and if I was going to get better I had to understand.

I washed my face off with cool water and looked in the mirror and saw the toll my awareness experience had taken. I had dark circles under my eyes, looked very thin, and had very little color in my face. I could run but no matter where I ran to, the awareness aftermath would also run with me. I had no choice but to hang in there a little longer. I had gotten very used to telling myself to hang in there one more hour, day, week, month.

I was accustomed to hearing myself say, "Just hold on and don't let go. Don't let yourself slip away. God is with me. His love and strength will get me through this weakness."

I made a cup of tea and sat in a wonderful, old, Queen Anne chair. I love Victorian furniture and I felt at home in that chair as the high back and wrapping arms held me. As silly as it sounded I felt safe in that chair for whatever reason. I sat wishing my dad was still alive and could be there to help me feel safe. But, it was just me and that chair.

My dad died from cancer just before my 21st birthday. I had experienced that same lost feeling—alone and scared—deep within my heart and soul when he passed away. And as I lay there on the operating table during my terrible ordeal, I had screamed in my head for him to help me somehow. I had beseeched God to let my dad help me in spirit to hold on. I felt it had worked then, and so thought it might work again. I felt like a lost

88

little girl instead of the grown woman I was. So, I began to do what I did, and still do, best—pray.

It was almost time for the meeting to begin, so I wrapped some ice cubes in a washcloth and placed it on my eyes to try and take away the puffiness. I hoped my bloodshot eyes would clear in the next half hour so that no one would know I had been crying.

Finally, it was time to go down to the meeting. My legs were shaking and my heart was pounding inside my chest, but I had to go. It was no longer an option.

I kept telling myself, "Just do it. Have faith and trust. I am not alone. It's going to be okay!"

In the symposium room there was a chair in the back by the door. I thought it was a good place for me, where no one would see me, just in case I felt like I had to run out. I was still very claustrophobic.

As the program began, one person started to tell the story of a movie called *The Doctor*. It was about a doctor who went through the motions of living until he became ill and became a patient himself.

He tied this into his speech about awareness and everyone started laughing and I thought, "They think this is funny?"

I was astonished to see how anyone could think it was funny. There is nothing funny about being sliced open while conscious. At that moment I felt myself gasping for air, and had an overwhelming urge to run out of there and never look back.

Then I felt a hand on my right shoulder and heard a voice speak my name, "Ms. Tracy?"

I jumped, and turned around to come face-to-face with Dr. Sebel. I thought he was upset with me, as if he had read my thoughts. He asked me to step out into the hallway.

I was frightened, but got up and followed him as he had asked. He said he had read my information and was sorry about what had happened to me. Then he asked me if I would like to speak to the audience about my experience of awareness. I was shocked. I was equally shocked when I said, "Yes."

I met Dr. Sebel and another anesthesiologist for lunch and we discussed my awareness experience.

After lunch, it was my time to speak. It was amazing to look across the room and see all those faces without masks. Then I began to speak from my heart and soul about what it felt like to experience awareness and how I felt as a human being. I could see their fear and discomfort as I continued to speak.

I did not stop until I heard myself say, "Thank you for staying to hear my story. I did this in order to help not only myself but each of you, too, because you hold so many lives in your hands. If you should ever have someone awake and in pain, I pray you'll remember this time today."

Everybody was moved—including me. Many in the audience wanted to stay and talk to me. Needless to say I was overwhelmed.

I spent the rest of the day talking to people until I was exhausted. I couldn't stand, think or speak. It was time for me to go home. I thanked Dr. Sebel for helping me finally find some answers.

For the second time since my ordeal, I had been given new hope. The first ray of hope had come from John Hess, and now the second had come through the symposium.

I left knowing without a doubt that something far greater than me and my experience was beginning to unfold.

CHAPTER 7

AWARE IS BORN
"Awareness With Anesthesia Research Education"

fter my return from the Atlanta symposium, I received many calls regarding awareness from anesthesiologists, Certified Registered Nurse Anesthetists (CRNAs), hospitals and reporters. I was asked repeatedly if I had a support group for people to contact. At the time I told them I did not, but assured them that I soon would, and in the meantime would be happy to help in anyway I could.

As the weeks rolled by the calls continued to come in, almost on a daily basis. Knowing that I had to do something more, I contacted a lawyer for advice on how to start a support group or foundation. The year was 1992.

We went over everything and then it came time to think of a name or appropriate acronym. AWARE was stuck in my mind.

"You have really been thinking about this, haven't you?" the lawyer said, smiling.

91

I smiled back and said, "No, not until this very moment."

"Well then, how did you come up with a word so fast?" he asked.

I responded, "I asked God and it just came out."

Of course we still needed to define the meaning of the acronym, AWARE, and what it could stand for. Again the words came out easily— *Awareness With Anesthesia Research Education.* Since that was what I was doing everyday of my life, it was perfect. AWARE it was—and is to this day.

Once the name was established, I developed the foundation's guidelines. The formal purpose of the AWARE foundation is to address the potentially serious problem of experiencing consciousness during surgery with or without recall of events and pain. Its goals are to:

- Increase the level of knowledge and understanding of the problem
- Develop methods for preventing and dealing with incidents
- Provide assistance to people who have experienced awareness
- Provide a clearinghouse and database for current literature and research findings
- Sponsor technical seminars for medical personnel
- Identify expert consultants to assist in resolving specific problems of awareness

When people called, it was almost like they thought AWARE was a big corporation with many employees. But AWARE consisted of just three—me, myself and I.

I turned my closet into an office. Even if the only thing in it was a desk and a file cabinet, I still had photos of my children, positive sayings hanging on the wall, and my cross above the phone and fax.

It wasn't much but it was mine and I was proud of my little space. More love and help came from that tiny office than from the big offices on

Wall Street. It was nothing and yet it was everything. I moved a few times through the years, but where I went AWARE was there also. My mission statement was simple:

> I founded AWARE in 1992 to educate the medical profession about the occurrence of awareness, and to provide training and self-help protocols for patients to prepare for successful surgical outcomes. AWARE is involved with research to discover a device that can let anesthesiologists and CRNAs know when awareness is occurring. AWARE supports successful surgeries and assists those who have experienced awareness while under anesthesia. There is help and hope at AWARE.

The first quarterly issue of the AWARE newsletter was distributed in December 1996 in an effort to educate the public about awareness and to be a source of support for patients who have experienced awareness. As AWARE gained momentum, phone calls and letters continued to increase. Selections from these letters are reprinted on the following pages. They not only represent the numerous messages that I have received, but also are an indicator of the success of the AWARE mission.

Dear Researchers,

While watching a program that told of the patients that had been awake during their operation, I felt compelled to write and add my story to the many I'm sure you will hear from.

About eight years ago, I went to the hospital for an elective surgery. I was not fearful because I was not ill and I had been told that you just relax and go to sleep and it seems like only minutes and the surgery is over. I didn't even consider that the "relax and go to sleep" part would be the most terrifying!

I was in the operating room, sitting up on my elbow on the table and chatting with the nurse when unknown to me the anesthesiologist came quietly in and injected something into my I.V. I told the nurse that I felt funny and fell back on the table. My eyes rolled up into my head, my body froze like cement and I couldn't breathe or speak. I could feel the nurse touch my face and I heard her tell me to take a deep breath, but I was helpless.

All I could move was my finger and in my mind I was screaming but no sound came out. I truly thought I was dying as I heard the nurse say, "Oh, you gave her the wrong one first."

Everything went black. As I came to in recovery, I tried to tell the nurse that something had gone wrong but I was so groggy that I fell back to sleep.

I woke up in my room with the doctor by my bed and he explained in a very light-hearted way how there was a little mistake and nothing to worry about. I fell asleep again and woke to find the heard nurse telling me that such a "reaction" affects about one in a million, "Lucky you!"

I felt confused and frightened about what had happened. I felt I had almost died and the doctors and nurses were joking about it. I wondered if I would have any medical side effects from such an experience but I could not get anyone to tell me anything beyond,

"Oh no. Don't worry about it."

I never did see the anesthesiologist, nor did he come and tell me what happened. I still feel the panic of feeling like I was dying when I think about the experience. I hope I never have to have surgery because I don't think I could face "going under" again. If you have any medical information on what happened to me and information on possible damage caused by such an experience I would appreciate it. Thank you for believing the patients and understanding their concerns.

Sincerely,
(name withheld)
Kitchener, Ontario Canada

Dear Sirs:

My experience was with the colonoscopy procedure which is excruciating, even though it is not actually surgery. (But they did remove some polyps.)

I had this procedure 4 years ago and I woke up in the middle of it in excruciating pain, I was screaming and the doctor yelled at me to lay still, which I could not, due to excruciating pain. Then I was nauseated and spent the day at the hospital. I was very sore throughout my colon for weeks. I really felt that my colon was damaged and lucky that it did not rupture. (I am 64 years old.)

When I went to his office a few weeks later for a check up he pretended that he did not know anything about my waking up.

I was supposed to go back in 3 years because I have a tendency and a family history of polyps which could become cancerous. I CANNOT force myself to go back. I am terrified, and also psychologically "freaked out" that I am afraid to go even to see another gastroenterologist.

PLEASE refer this letter to someone who can advise me medically. Is there a chance that spinal anesthesia could be used to control pain during a colonoscopy? I was supposed to have another one a year ago. Please tell me if a "spinal" would work.

I am risking cancer I am told. PLEASE help me.

Sincerely,
(name withheld)
Lewiston, Maine

To Whom it May Concern:

Our office represents a victim of intraoperative awareness during a face lift and a brow lift. The defendant doctors have indicated that instances of intraoperative awareness are so rare that it was not necessary to inform the patient of the possibility that this might occur during this elective surgery.

The existence of your organization, in addition to research I have conducted, tends to refute the defendant doctors' claims. I would be interested in any information you could provide regarding the frequency and/or circumstances of these occurrences and any medical experts who are particularly knowledgeable about these occurrences.

Very truly yours,
(name withheld)
Santa Ana, California

Gentlemen:

A family member took down your organization's name and address from a radio spot, and passed it on to me. He inferred that your organization is either conducting research or acting in support of people who have experienced ineffective anesthesia coverage during surgery.

I had such an experience in 1985 during the surgical birth of my son. If it is true that you are somehow involved with this topic, I would be most interested to learn more about your group and its purpose.

Please send me any available written materials, or telephone me. I can be reached during business hours and at home. I hope to hear from you.

> Very truly yours,
> (name withheld)
> New Freedom, Pennsylvania

Dear AWARE President:

It was a pleasure to know you from the ASA newsletter, Oct. 1994.

Would you please kindly let me know if there is an update recommended standard as well as any monitoring for detection as well as prevention on intraoperative awareness under general anesthesia, in presence of pain or without pain. Many thanks.

Best regards.

Sincerely,
Professor (name withheld)
Beijing
People's Republic of China

Dear Jeanette,

It was nice to talk with you last Friday night. How good it felt to talk to someone that could understand what I had gone through during surgery.

My experience of being awake during surgery was in January 1983. The doctors were operating on me for a hysterectomy. During that time they found a problem with my liver and called in another doctor. They did the hysterectomy and repaired the liver and also took out my appendix. During this time or when they had finished, I somehow was awakened. The pain was excruciating, felt like my torso was on fire. My eyes opened or were lifted open by the anesthesiologist because at that time he said, "Look, she's wide awake." The doctor was (ethnicity identified) and I recognized his voice.

I remember screaming and screaming and nobody heard me or came to my aid. I was helpless and couldn't move. There were two nurses working around the table I was on. I could hear them talking and could not believe they didn't notice what I was going through. I looked for a clock on the wall and didn't see one. The next thing I remember was a feeling of warmth over me and the pain was gone.

After telling my doctor about what happened, the anesthesiologist came to my room a couple of days later. I told him what happened during surgery.

He said, "I wake up all my patients the same." He was arrogant and didn't care about my feelings. I couldn't believe what he said and that made me angry. The reason I did not sue the anesthesiologist was because I did not want to involve the other doctors.

Although the doctors believed me, I was never given a satisfactory explanation. I have asked the surgeons to never have that particular anesthesiologist work with them if I ever have anymore surgeries. They have complied as I have had two minor surgeries since that time without any problem.

Over the years, I have had times when I awake with strong feelings of claustrophobia. With positive thinking, I have learned to deal with this.

I hope through your efforts that someday soon no one will have to experience what you and many others have endured.

Thank you so much Jeanette for listening and understanding. You have my permission to use my experience in your work.

God Bless You,
(name withheld)

Dear Sirs,

I was born with club feet which were corrected at birth through surgeries and braces. However, as the years passed by and I reached the age of 40, my feet began to turn backwards once again. My orthopedic surgeon refers to it as "Adult Club Feet."

Over the past few years I have had 9 surgeries on my feet (5 on the left and 4 on the right), one knee surgery and one back surgery for two herniated disks.

I woke up during the 5th or 6th surgery on my feet. I even woke up during a dental procedure. My anesthesiologist told my husband and I the medical term for what I have is called "awareness." Prior to awakening during the surgery (the left ankle ball and socket were removed, repaired and replaced) I needed no pre-op for surgeries. Now I do.

My question to your Foundation is, "Do you know if there is a way to alert the anesthesiologist and physicians that you are awake?"

Thank God I had some medical background in my career. I have worked in surgery, so I had no fears of surgery. None until I awoke during one. I knew I had to. I remembered instruments called for, conversations, music played before I'd convince them I had been awake. I counted my pulse from the pulse oximeter. It was 33. Paralyzed, I was still aware of the plastic breathing tube of the ventilator and the O_2 being puffed into my lungs.

I bared down as hard as I possibly could. This made my pulse jump from 33 to 78. The anesthesiologist bent down over my head and saw that my eyes were open about halfway. He then kissed me on the forehead and said, "Good night, sweetheart."

I repeated over and over and over again, "I woke up. I felt him cut me." I did this until both the orthopedic surgeon and anesthesiologist came into my recovery room.

The anesthesiologist did not charge for that surgery. I did not sue because it isn't my nature plus I acknowledge the fact that doctors are not God. Besides how could they know I had "awareness" when I myself didn't know—until it happened to me. Thank God my medical background gave me the sense of calmness I needed to have the sense to make my pulse oximeter jump as fast as I could as quickly as possible.

Not only does the public need to be educated on "awareness" but also on how to prevent it and/or stop it should it happen to them or a loved one.

Now prior to any surgery, I request a conference with the anesthesiologist. I have him mark it on my chart as if I was allergic to a medication. Now I *have* to have a pre-op before any surgery. People with awareness need to know what to do should this happen to them and how to prevent it or stop it.

We need some form of card or bracelet stating we have "awareness" in case of a wreck, loss of consciousness, etc.—like a diabetic bracelet.

Early this month I found out I have to have yet another surgery on my left foot. My physician knows I have to have 60 to 90 days to gather enough courage for surgery. I've scheduled it twice and cancelled both times. I truly wouldn't wish this on my worst enemy. I have no idea where to seek help emotionally for this. Any and all suggestions would be greatly appreciated. I shall anxiously await your reply.

Sincerely,
(name withheld)
Lubbock, Texas

To Whom It May Concern:

My wife recently had open-heart surgery. Upon recovery she claims to have felt and heard everything, and is very detailed in her description of the procedure.

She is now unable to sleep without nightmares related to her surgery and *will not* consider any other procedures in the future.

Please send us any information you may have that might provide my dear wife with some comfort.

Sincerely,
(name withheld)
Moses Lake, Washington

CHAPTER 8

PASSAGE TO
FREEDOM
"What we don't know can hurt us."

I n 1993, CNN invited me to Atlanta to do a television program after another symposium. I returned to Emory University and we taped at Crawford-Lawton Hospital. As we walked beside a beautiful lake, the reporter asked me about my story. She seemed in awe as I told it to her. She said she had spoken to someone on the anesthesia side who told her that awareness was very rare and that other circumstances and complications prior to surgery were primarily responsible for its occurrence. I told her that none of them applied to me. I informed her that I was so healthy when I went in for surgery that I didn't even have the hernia for which I was operated on. I was still early into my recovery, so I was defensive. I said that I would meet with anyone who told her it was a rare occurrence to discuss the matter.

It was a sunny afternoon and very hot in Atlanta. I was facing into the sun, which made it difficult to see. In the middle of the interview I began flashing back to the operating table. As I was squinting I began seeing the color red from the bright sunlight. At the time, red was very frightening and alarming to me. The effect was similar to that of the operating room lights above me while my eyes were paralyzed shut. I started to shake and tremble and thought I was going to pass out. We took a break so I could catch my breath, and I reminded myself of where I was.

Everything was okay and most of all I was safe.

We continued the interview and the reporter asked me to describe what I felt was happening to me during the flashback. It was as if she and her crew wanted to capture the disaster that was happening in my mind. I explained how the red light had triggered the memory of the operating room. I said that I needed some time to collect my thoughts, and left to be by myself for a little while. I knew what I needed to do for myself and that's what I did. I was feeling more and more in control of myself, despite the tendency to flash back. I figured they could wait for me if they wanted. They did. We continued and everything went fine from there.

After filming, I climbed into the van with the crew. As we drove we began again to talk about what had happened to me. Once they heard the details of my story I could see the transformation taking place in their minds. The reporter asked what I would recommend to others who might face surgery someday. I advised her that the first thing patients should do is talk to their anesthesia provider before going under and let the provider know about their concerns. Second, they should be sure that the provider will stay with them throughout the surgery. Third, they should find out if they need to have a muscle relaxant—if they need to be paralyzed. Fourth, I suggested that they find out if it is necessary to undergo general anesthesia or if a regional or local anesthetic would work as well, or even better. These are things I never thought of before my hernia operation.

The rest of the crew had questions that I answered. They dropped me off at my hotel and thanked me for the interview. The reporter said to me, "Jeanette, you're doing a wonderful job for the world. Keep it up." That meant a lot to me. I've met many reporters who were only concerned about getting their story.

That night I wondered whether I was doing the right thing. The CNN crew had had such a strong reaction when I told them my story and walked them through the nightmare of the operating room, that I wondered how it may have changed their lives.

Then I thought, "When people see this around the country what will it do to them?" I had a cup of tea and sat in a big lean-back chair gazing across the room. I decided that I had to be doing the right thing. If I didn't continue, then my message would be lost and awareness would be hidden once again. If anything was going to change, I couldn't be silent. It might make people uncomfortable but the experience itself wouldn't be nearly as devastating to victims if they knew the possibility existed. I was taken by surprise during my operation, and that was surely more frightening than if I had known awareness could happen. This was a journey I needed to remain on. Nothing would

The reporter asked what I would recommend to others who might face surgery someday.

I advised her that the first thing patients should do is talk to their anesthesia provider before going under and let the provider know about their concerns.

Second, they should be sure that the provider will stay with them throughout the surgery.

Third, they should find out if they need to have a muscle relaxant—if they need to be paralyzed.

Fourth, I suggested that they find out if it is necessary to undergo general anesthesia or if a regional or local anesthetic would work as well, or even better.

change unless someone changed things. I prayed to God for guidance and strength, and that the reporters I come in contact with in the future will keep in mind what this is really about—helping others, not doctor bashing or hospital bashing. It's about letting others know what could happen in the worst of circumstances. Knowledge is power. What we don't know can hurt us.

The following day, I met with Dr. Sebel and four CRNAs at Emory. I asked them, "Are you comfortable with me letting people know that there is a possibility awareness could happen to them? Or do you think what I'm doing is wrong?"

They all agreed that awareness is a problem and said, "If anyone can change it, we think you can." That was the confirmation I needed. The right thing to do was to stay on the path and continue the mission. And that's what I've been doing.

In 1994, I was contacted by a *Washington Post* reporter who wanted to interview me. I agreed. The reporter came to my home and he and I talked about awareness as the photographer set up his camera and lights. I thought that it was going well until we got to the point when the reporter wanted to know the name of the anesthesiologist and the hospital involved with my awareness experience. I told him that the surgery took place in October 1990 in Texas, and that the names he was seeking were not important. The reporter kept pressing me. He told me that if it wasn't a big deal, and if I was telling the truth, then I would name the anesthesiologist and the hospital. Because I had never taken any settlement money, he said I was able to speak freely about it, including naming those involved. I said it was a personal decision I had made not to reveal their identities. I have held them in confidence to this day.

He continued to badger me for the next 25 minutes. I realized I would either have to give him the information he wanted or ask him to leave my home. I wasn't quite sure which I would choose. I was still very green as far as dealing with the media, and I didn't want to upset anyone or hurt anyone's feelings. Plus, I was still in a vulnerable state of mind.

I found the strength to look the reporter in the eye and tell him, "I have asked you to please respect my wishes, and you continue to ask me over and over and over, so I have to ask you to leave my home now."

The reporter looked at me and said, "I'm a reporter for the *Washington Post*. Do you know what that means?"

I replied, "I'm the only person who's trying to make a difference here. Do you know what that means?" On that note the reporter slammed his folder closed, abruptly got up and told his photographer, "Come on, let's get out of here." They packed up and left.

As they were leaving, the photographer turned around and looked at me. He didn't say a word but gave me a thumbs up.

I was worried what they might say and how I would be perceived afterward, but it was something I needed to do. That reporter hadn't gone through what I had, and he wasn't trying to do something to correct the problem the way I was. He was looking for a story and that was it.

The following year, I was contacted by a different reporter from *The Washington Post*. This time the story ran.

I continued my journey and was invited to more symposiums to speak on awareness. I attended a symposium in San Francisco with a group of CRNAs. I had no idea what to expect. I was amazed at how friendly and understanding the nurse anesthetists were. They were there to help and I was accepted by them with open arms.

No matter what questions I had, the CRNAs answered them. I was given details, and if there was something I didn't understand, they made it clear that it was okay to ask for more information. Whatever it took, they

I finished my story and asked for questions. I thought there might be two or three. The audience was filled with outstretched arms.

were ready to teach me. I was touched by their compassion.

I attended a lecture in which I was able to listen to people speak about awareness during anesthesia, and I was surprised by the openness with which they spoke. I have never taken so many notes in my life. When it came time for me to speak, I was introduced by the symposium leader who was very emotional and talked about me like we were old friends. I was moved. I thought to myself, "My God, these people really do care about what happened to me. And they don't want it to happen to others."

I was choked up before I ever took the stage. I was not only among colleagues, I was among friends. I looked around and the room was quiet. You could hear a pin drop. I hoped someone would cough or get up for a drink of water. It was as if they were glued to their chairs.

When the introduction was over, I rose from my seat as the audience began to applaud. I walked up the steps to the platform and as I was standing there looking at all the faces, I could almost read their minds.

I told my story, as usual, and nobody stirred. Then, at one point, I saw people begin to wipe their eyes. They really did care. They really wanted to learn more. They truly understood.

I finished my story and asked for questions. I thought there might be two or three. The audience was filled with outstretched arms. "Where do I begin," I thought. I didn't know if I was supposed to call on them or if there was someone else to do that. So I just decided I would start at the front of the room and work my way back.

As we communicated, nothing was held back. Everyone there wanted to know what was the best way to handle an awareness situation—what to say, what to do—and whether they should go back and share what they just learned. One gentleman asked me three or four questions because he said he didn't know when he would have a chance to see me again.

I could have stayed all night. It was a rare opportunity for them to be able to question an awareness patient. I was in a unique position to explain the things they didn't know firsthand, and that I knew so well. I decided to give a demonstration. I asked for a tie or a napkin to cover my eyes. I walked them through it. We all closed our eyes, and I asked them to get inside themselves—to feel very small and trapped within their own bodies. People began to quiver, tremble and even cry. I was ready for people to get up and walk out. But nobody left. They all stayed.

I wrapped up late, taking time from the following speaker, because I was asked to continue answering a few more questions. The audience wanted to hear more. When the next lecturer finished, I was approached by a crowd of people. There was so much interest in the topic. Some asked me to come to their hospitals or to speak at luncheons. The symposium was such a positive environment. I was no longer alone on the path. There were loving, caring individuals trying to achieve the same goal I was.

When I got home my answering machine was filled with messages from nurse anesthetists asking questions. People offered to pay the charges for my return call. Many of my biases toward the medical community changed because of the consideration of those CRNAs.

As I copied down the list of people who had left messages, I ran across a few who had asked what they could do to help me. One of the things I needed was help with the correspondence and phone calls that I was handling all by myself.

A few women came to meet me at my home in Alexandria, Virginia. We sat down and put together a plan. In addition to taking care of

I have encountered anesthesiologists who have told me that they've never had a patient experience awareness. "How would you know?" I always ask. "Have you ever asked a patient what was the last thing he or she remembered before going out, and what was the first thing he or she recalled upon waking up?" It's hardly a typical question.

AWARE, I was dealing with the stresses of a marriage that was falling apart. I was on my own and going through a divorce. I had no idea how to manage. There were some rough months that followed. But I asked God to guide me through it and to send me help. And, whenever I asked for help, a nurse anesthetist would come along. There were plenty of anesthesiologists that were involved in my work as well, such as Dr. Sebel, but the nurse anesthetists were always there. They became my new family.

Over the years, I have learned that many anesthesiologists believe they have a more important role in the anesthesia process simply because they are physicians. In reality, anesthesiologists and CRNAs adhere to the same code of standards, have comparable anesthesia-related educations, and do the same things when it comes to administering anesthetics to patients and monitoring their vital signs.

I have encountered anesthesiologists who have told me that they've never had a patient experience awareness. "How would you know?" I always ask. "Have you ever asked a patient what was the last thing he or she remembered before going out, and what was the first thing he or she recalled upon waking up?" It's hardly a typical question.

The nurse anesthetists I've known over the years have impressed me with their curiosity and their willingness to learn. I believe the best anesthesia provider for the job—nurse anesthetist or anesthesiologist—is the one who is most sensitive to the patient's needs. That means the provider who is open, honest, and most genuinely concerned about the patient's well being, rather than being focused on misrepresentation or being sued.

The awareness victims I have worked with have never stated that they were seeking answers because of money. Like me, the most important thing for these victims is to know what happened to them, and why.

CHAPTER 9

MAINSTREAM MEDIA EXPOSURE REVEALS THE TRUTH

"...willingness to speak out."

I n 1995, I was interviewed by *Inside Edition.* For nearly four months afterward I was flooded with calls. My phone bill skyrocketed. I received many requests for information concerning awareness. So I went to the library to collect information to put together packets that I sent out. I remembered how important it was to me when I received that first piece of paper about awareness from my therapist. I got requests not only from awareness sufferers, but from people confronting a future surgery as well.

On May 1 of that same year, the *Boston Globe* ran an article titled, "This is No Time to Wake Up, But Many Do."[1] It stated that medical tech-

115

nology had no means of discovering the level of consciousness of a patient. On that subject, Dr. Daniel Carr, an anesthesiologist at New England Medical Center, said, "That's why the awareness issue has become so important. The only clues for an anesthetist are physical symptoms, such as tears, increased heart rate, and blood pressure."

Later that year, the *Inside Edition* story ran again due to popular demand. Because of the tremendous response to the *Inside Edition* segment, I had to ask some friends to help me with all the mail that poured in. At the end of this chapter is a selection from the several hundred letters I received after the segment aired.

I was at a point now where my finances were dwindling away. My phone bill had soared to almost $1,400 per month. About 85 percent of the people who called were awareness patients themselves, the other 15 percent were people who wanted to know more about it.

I went to my jewelry box and scattered the contents on the bed. I had to sell my jewelry in order to continue making phone calls and sending mail. I started working more hours. I did whatever I had to do to keep AWARE available for those who needed help.

In 1996 I did more taping. I was physically and mentally drained. I dropped down to 116 pounds. I hadn't weighed that since I was 14 or 15 years old. I wasn't sleeping or eating the way I should have been. I got sick. I was constantly troubled with colds, flu, and bronchial pneumonia.

I cut back on my grocery shopping and my heat. I cocooned myself in blankets that winter and looked forward to getting into my car and turning on the heat on my way to work.

When I think back on everything I went through at the time to get things done I don't know if it was wise. But AWARE had become larger than just myself. I had listened to so many people crying and begging on the phone. Families that were lost and broken. I knew all about what they were experiencing, having gone through it myself. I couldn't allow that to happen to anyone. But I had to ask myself, "How can I help all these people?"

I cut back on my own personal life in hopes that I would find the strength to carry on. It was extremely difficult because I was sick all the time. Once I went to work with a 103-degree fever and had to keep covering my face with powder so no one would see the redness in my cheeks or the beads of sweat. I fainted one day from sheer exhaustion. I had chest pain and chronic fatigue. My dreams would be interrupted by nightmares in which I was trapped and frozen and my screams went unheard.

The doctors asked me why I allowed this to happen to me. I cried and said that there was nobody else to do the work I was doing and that I had to keep going or more lives would be lost. "How could I stop?" I asked.

I was taken from work to the hospital because of dehydration. I was mentally and physically exhausted. The doctor asked me why I allowed this to happen. I cried and said that there was nobody else to do the work I was doing and that I had to keep going or more lives would be lost. "How could I stop?" I asked. I had no one to turn to. No one to talk to. I didn't want anyone at work to know what I was going through. I had to perform at my best at all times.

I told the doctor to release me so I could get back to work. He said he was thinking of keeping me overnight and maybe for two or three days. I was alarmed. Having been sick with pneumonia and the flu, I couldn't afford to miss another day of work. If I missed another day of work, I missed another meal. I missed electricity. I had more candles in my home than St. Peter's Cathedral. I was doing all I possibly could. My jewelry collection was shrinking, my art pieces and antiques that I cherished so much were disappearing from my home.

There were times I prayed for help and times I almost gave up. Although I was grateful for being blessed with the ability to help others and change things, I needed someone to help me. I was broke.

I had brought media attention to the issue of anesthetic awareness, had lectured at symposiums to doctors and nurses, and had worked with thousands of patients, and now I was on the verge of being homeless, penniless, and hungry. Where was I going to go? What was I going to do? I was a bag of bones. I was wearing I size two. My daughter, Lisa, wore a size two. I couldn't afford to buy new clothes, so I altered the ones I had. I had dark circles under my eyes that I had to cover every day. I wasn't eating, I wasn't sleeping, and all I could think was, "My God, what have I done?" I had sacrificed myself in every area of my life without realizing it.

One of my greatest fears was that my phone might be turned off. I would walk through my house and wonder what I could sell next. I was so afraid of not having enough money for postage stamps or for photocopies that I sold more of my belongings. I worked longer. I was asked to do some counseling. It was great for me. A friend from work wanted to put together a group of women. We met together at my house and everyone would bring a dish. I kept a container for donations. It was great on two counts: I could eat and I could collect enough money to mail more packets when people asked for them.

God has never let me down. I would cry and pray and speak out loud about my fears and concerns. I would ask for protection and guidance and help. As the old adage goes, "Be careful what you wish for, you just might get it." So what happened next? I was contacted by a reporter who wanted to do a story for *Redbook* magazine. It would be my first major magazine piece.

I spoke to a wonderful writer named Michael, who was kind and considerate. He was very interested in my story but he was also interested in my current situation. I was able to speak freely with him and it helped me tremendously. I told him all about my financial predicament and my poor health.

Michael asked the normal questions that were usually asked during my interviews. He also asked what I thought when I realized I was still in the operating room. I said that when I was unable to swallow or breathe for myself, I knew I was in trouble and had to fight like hell to let someone know I was awake.

He asked, "So, Jeanette, you couldn't breathe for yourself nor move or speak?"

I responded, "No, Michael, everything that we take for granted, like breathing, opening our eyes and moving, was gone. I was buried alive inside myself. Michael, I really thought I was going to die."

I began to cry and Michael's voice became soft as he said, "I'm so sorry this happened to you, but what you're doing is going to help many people."

I knew he was right and I explained, "Michael, it was very hard, but today my tears are simply about being blessed with life. I'm alive and now as long as I am alive, I have one hell of a good chance to change this problem."

He then asked what I could remember about the surgery. I began to talk him through the cutting of my flesh, and how I smelled and felt my flesh burning. I told him about the songs I sung in my head, the yelling and praying, and most of all, fighting to live. He became quiet and I asked if he was okay. He said, "Yes, I'm okay. I'm just thinking of what hell it must have been for you. Jeanette, I'm really sorry it happened."

I said, "Well, Michael, this is your part of this whole picture with me. God gave you this story to do, because it's going to touch millions of lives and you'll be shocked how many people will surface after this story comes out. I thank you and everyone at *Redbook*."

I knew he understood completely what I was going through and what I was trying to accomplish.

After the *Redbook* interview, I was called by a TV producer from *Dateline* in March of 1996. I was asked if I was interested in doing a show.

As I spoke with all of the reporters, I was amazed by their reaction to my story. It was clear they had never heard of anesthetic awareness, and I thought this was odd considering they were reporters. I wondered to myself, "Where has everybody been all this time?"

Once the *Dateline* show aired, again the phone and mail came non-stop. I would stay up all night writing back to awareness patients and others needing more information. I wondered how the program would affect the lives of those who hadn't known about the subject. I thought about the patients who were worse off than I was and couldn't afford to call me or even mail me a letter to get answers.

In 1997, while I was still working and running the AWARE foundation, I started speaking at hospitals. Nurse anesthetists were eager to help me even more. I knew I had a lifeline to them and with them. I remember telling a good friend of mine, Rita Rupp, a registered nurse who worked for the American Association of Nurse Anesthetists (AANA), that I was scared because I didn't know how I was going to get by. I had already sold 75 percent of everything I owned.

But I knew that I was doing something that needed to be done and the AANA was going to be a big part of it. I didn't know how, I only knew I had to do my best in every way I could, including my personal life.

Again, I was contacted by another television producer. He worked for *Extra*. That was December 1997. It was cold in Alexandria, Virginia, just like the previous winter.

When the reporters came to my home, it was once again turned into a studio made for television. My living room was moved out and redone as a set-up stage. Black paper was taped over the windows to cut the glare from the sun and snow. Studio lights went up and on. And again I was shooting another story on awareness under anesthesia.

As I sat there thinking of the millions of people who would see this program, I was again grateful for the opportunity and for everyone at *Extra* for making this effort. We began and the memories flooded my mind and the hearts of the *Extra* crew. Again the familiar words I've heard before came from their mouths: "I never heard of this. What a nightmare! Thank you for speaking out."

One of the cameramen asked, "What if you needed surgery again, what would you do?"

I looked at him, hiding my fear, and smiled and said, "I would have you in there with me taping it."

I thanked them for their help and off they went. After the program aired, the phone calls, letters and cries for help started immediately. I just kept telling myself, "Who knows better than you?" So, by helping them, I was not only helping myself to heal but also helping others to heal.

The phone calls and letters never stopped. Word was spreading, and mainstream media was focusing on the topic.

Then I was contacted by *Time* magazine. *Redbook* was unbelievable for me. That was the first article. But now *Time* magazine was interested in doing a story and they wanted to know my opinion on so many different things.

MAINSTREAM MEDIA EXPOSURE REVEALS THE TRUTH

The *Time* magazine article was titled, "What's Up, Doc?"[2] It described awareness as "every surgery patient's nightmare," and contained the statement, "You're awake enough to feel the knife but not enough to scream." The article said that "These unexpected wake-ups occur in at least 40,000 of the nation's 20 million annual surgeries, according to Emory University anesthesiologist Peter Sebel." I thought, "Bravo. Now we have an anesthesiologist who is speaking the truth and isn't afraid to bring it out!" The numbers were amazing to me—40,000 surgeries annually! It may not seem like a lot compared to 20 million, but that's 40,000 human lives altered every year. And some believe that's a low estimate. But even if the number was 1,000 or 100 or 1, it is still a human life—a person who has been tortured, traumatized, broken, confused, scared, made helpless and phobic.

The *Time* article revealed additional information about awareness and survivors of the problem. It cited one study that suggested only 35 percent of those who experienced awareness ever said anything. Most anesthesiologists had no conception of how deeply their patients had suffered. Personally, I have talked with countless people who wanted to keep their experiences quiet. They didn't want anyone to know. They were afraid of people thinking they were crazy, not being able to get life insurance, losing their jobs, being judged, and losing loved ones. We know there are approximately 40,000 cases each year, but we don't know how many people experience awareness and never admit to it.

In the article, Dr. Charles McKlesky, an anesthesiologist at Texas A&M, admitted, "I used to think people who talked about this topic were flakes."[2] He became a believer after one of his patients told him everything that was said while he was under anesthesia. Since then, Dr. McKlesky has done a lot of work to reveal the truth about awareness, and like Dr. Sebel has written many articles on the topic.

I learned a lot from the *Time* magazine article. Maybe that's why it has stayed in my mind for so long. I realized that the humiliation of anesthetic awareness, caused in part by callous comments and actions of healthcare personnel in the OR, is not just reserved for women. I had a patient, a man, who woke up during surgery, like the tens of thousands that do each year. He woke up to find a female nurse holding up his penis and laughing.

At the end of the article, the writer mentioned that when an awareness victim comes out of surgery it is natural that the patient will feel like the only person in the world who has experienced this. That's how I felt after my surgery. The emptiness was so intense.

That's why AWARE had to exist. I had to keep my phone on. I had to be there everyday for the new patients. Day after day, year after year.

Without a doubt, 1998 was a breathtaking year for me. So much happened that I was shocked. I was working and I had a page to call a woman named Lisa. So I called the woman when I had a break. I spoke to a wonderful young lady. She said she was a television producer and wanted to know if it was possible to interview me. I told her sure. Then I asked who she worked for.

"Oprah Winfrey," she said.

I thought it was a joke. I had kept saying for the past year that I was going to be on Oprah, so I thought someone was playing a practical joke on me.

So I said, "Really? Well, how is Oprah?"

"She's fine," the woman said. "When would be a good time for us to talk?"

"Well, when would you like to talk?" I replied, keeping my sense of humor.

I continued, "Let's talk now. Is Oprah busy today? Maybe she can meet me for lunch?"

"Excuse me?" she said, after hearing the sarcasm in my voice.

"My name is Lisa and I really am from *The Oprah Winfrey Show*. And Ms. Winfrey would like you to be a guest on the show," she politely asserted. When she said that her voice changed and became very sincere.

I knew now that this was it. This was my dream come true. This was what I had been praying and asking God for. It was happening. I asked Lisa if it would be okay for me to call back after work. I was trembling. I wanted to jump up and down and sing and shout. But I had to contain myself until I got to the AWARE office at my home. Then I let it all out. I was so excited. God really did answer my prayers. Now there was no stopping. I finally calmed myself down. I just kept thinking: Oprah. A woman who has made her voice heard throughout the world. Certainly she could help me help others.

That evening I couldn't get home fast enough. I remember looking out over the Chesapeake Bay and watching the lights dance across the water. I watched the planes fly into Ronald Reagan International Airport and thought to myself that I was not alone anymore. And I truly believed for the first time, without a shadow of a doubt, that I hadn't even been alone on that operating room table.

Faith reminded me of that. We all have our own beliefs, and I respect everyone's right to believe as they wish. I base my life on my own beliefs. Without that higher power, I myself would be powerless. When I think back on the Oprah episode, "Finding Your Spirit," I can't help but marvel at how aptly titled it was.

Our spirits are beyond who we think we are. My spirit had been broken after my surgery. But we can mend our spirits and make them even stronger than before, if we just believe that we are never alone.

After the excitement of the *The Oprah Winfrey Show*, I got another call from Lisa. Instead of going to Chicago, however, I was invited to Texas. At that point in time, Oprah was going through her own battle in the form of a lawsuit. So I had no problem going down to Texas. I just hoped it wasn't too close to where my surgery had been. I flew to Amarillo to do a show on Ash Wednesday. I will never forget it. As a Catholic, Ash Wednesday is an important day for me. I requested that someone drive me to a church. I wasn't shooting the program until that afternoon, so I spent the morning praying and giving thanks. Before every lecture, show, interview, symposium, and surgery I am present for, I sit and pray. I always start by thanking God for everything I've been through and all that I'm becoming. I ask only to be an instrument to touch the lives of every person I come in contact with. I ask to remain honest and grounded. I make myself ready to be used in anyway that God wants.

That day in the church I was able to receive communion, get down on my knees, gaze at the cross, and cry tears of joy. As I prayed someone in the pew behind me placed his hand on my shoulder, and in a sweet, gentle, frail voice, I heard a man behind me say, "He knows, child. He knows." I turned around and I took his hand and kissed it. I smiled at him with tears streaming down my smiling face and I agreed with his words.

"Isn't it great," I said. He took my hand and kissed it. He knelt down, made the sign of the cross, and then quietly shuffled away.

I went back to my hotel and when I got there one of Oprah's bodyguards was waiting for me. As I got out of the car he asked me if I was aware that they'd been looking for me. I replied "No." "Well, you just can't take off like that," he said. I asked why not, because the taping wasn't for another hour and a half.

"You're a public figure now," he told me.

I said, "No, I'm just me. I'm no one special. I'm just Jeanette." I thanked him for being concerned. I also told him that God was watching over me. He smiled.

MAINSTREAM MEDIA EXPOSURE REVEALS THE TRUTH

I took a hot bubble bath and had a cup of my favorite Earl Gray tea. I got dressed after about 15 outfit changes. In the end, I chose something basic. I was taken backstage and I met Naomi Judd. John Travolta was there, too. Oprah introduced herself, read the information, and shook her head. Then she said in her charismatic manner, "My God, girl, you've been through a lot." And I agreed but told her things were going to get better. I knew this was neither the beginning nor the end, but would last for as long as God wanted it to.

In the audience that day was Dr. McKlesky. When I told my story the audience was stunned. Dr. McKlesky told the audience that the problem of anesthetic awareness was being handled.

During the break, Oprah leaned over, held my hand, and said, "How did you make it through that?"

I replied, "Oprah, I remember lying there and thinking, 'I can't die because no one will ever know that I was awake and I will die alone,' and I don't ever want to die alone." She looked at me with tears in her eyes and said, "Oh, my God." When we came back from the break Oprah told the audience that we had just been talking and mentioned that there was something that I should tell everyone. Oprah was too choked up to even speak. So I repeated what I had said and the reaction of the audience was the same as Oprah's. Clearly, that connection with her audience is why she's so successful at what she does.

Later that year I was invited to appear on *The Leeza Show*. The host, Leeza Gibbons, is a wonderful, kind woman. She is so "present" in her interviews. Before the taping she shared with me her fears of this happening to her someday, and wanted to know if I would help the others on that day's show because the topic was medical mishaps. Of course, I was happy to do that.

I was relaxed as we started the show. After I shared my awareness story, others told their stories. I was struck by the realization that what it all

126

comes down to is for each of us to take charge of our bodies and lives.

I was approached to do the *Tom Snyder Show.* I had heard various rumors about him conducting tough interviews and didn't really know what to expect. We were shooting late at night for the first time in my life. I had dinner with a friend who asked me if I was nervous, and I confessed that I was. But Tom proved to be a real gentleman, and even reminded me of my dad. He seemed very protective, understood what I was trying to accomplish, and was very helpful.

One of my next interviews appeared in *U.S. News and World Report.* In this article, Dr. Anthony Messina, an anesthesiologist, stated that at the age of 7 he experienced his own awareness during surgery.[3]

Dr. Messina and I have talked numerous times since that article appeared, and we agree that possibly hundreds of thousands of people experience awareness during surgery, taking into consideration vast numbers of unreported cases. This is in stark contrast to a statement in the article that awareness is thought to be uncommon!

Interestingly, the article also stated that research conducted by University of Chicago Hospital anesthesiologists revealed that compounds called solanaceous glycoalkaloids, which are found in foods like potatoes and tomatoes, can slow the metabolism of local anesthestics and muscle relaxants in the body.[3]

I did other newspaper interviews, as well as interviews for *Allure* and *People* magazines. In the *People* feature, I was pictured attending to and comforting a patient undergoing surgery. The caption quoted me as saying, "We should know when someone is in pain."

In 1998, the positive, forward momentum of AWARE continued. I will forever be grateful for all the support I received that year. I wasn't just on a roll, I was living my dream and keeping my word to God to make a difference.

To Whom It May Concern:

On Thursday, January 26, 1995 on "Inside Edition" I was made aware that I was not the only person who had such a terrible, or for a better word, "horrifying" and "painful" experience during surgery.

On October 7, 1987 I was admitted to lipectomy surgery at _____ hospital in Toronto, Ontario, Canada. I was the first patient to enter the OR (operating room) that morning and was very excited about the new "m" that would evolve from this procedure. I had had liposuction in 1985-86 and was familiar with the post-operative results and the procedure itself. Anesthetic was administered to me in the usual manner—injectable—and there was a "blank" (like I passed out) and then I was awakening again!

Panic stricken but could not move a finger, wink an eye, move my nose or whatever part of my body I would like to move. I could hear my surgeon coming into the OR and saying, "Is she out?"

I thought, "Oh my God, he's going to start cutting into me and suctioning and I'm awake."

Someone was playing with my fingers. I tried to squeeze or move my fingers. I couldn't. I tried to move my eyelids and even tried to smile despite the situation. It was not working. I was screaming to them in my mind wondering why they couldn't hear me.

I felt the scalpel cut into my skin deeply and felt the burn from it too. I heard my surgeon say, "She is mostly concerned about her ass," and proceeded further.

Eventually, maybe 15 or 20 minutes later, I passed out and became conscious in the recovery room. I told my doctor and the nurses what had happened. He was shocked when I repeated his exact words. I became weaker and fainting started. I also became incontinent (lost control of my bladder, urinating on the floor while unconscious). The nurses were very concerned and insisted I remain overnight under close observation. My anesthesiologist gave me an injection about 9 p.m. and vomiting ceased and I later fell asleep.

Upon awakening the next morning, October 8, I was informed that two other ladies who were second and third in the OR on October 7 were also sick but I did not know if they were aware of their surgery as well. One of the nurses said it was anesthetic poisoning. Maybe so...

I would really like to know what happened to me that day. Why did I not become fully anesthetized? Why was I aware of my surgery?

This experience has left me afraid (petrified) to have surgery under anesthetic for the rest of my life.

I am so happy that doctors are aware of this horrible occurrence and that they are trying to solve the puzzle.

If I can personally be of any help, please do not hesitate to contact me.

Sincerely,
(name withheld)
London, Ontario, Canada

I saw an episode on "Inside Edition" about awareness. I, like the two people shown on Inside Edition, have experienced the terror of coming "to" during surgery. But, unlike the two featured on "Inside Edition", I was told there would be a possibility of this happening before I underwent surgery.

I was in a precarious situation. I had undergone open-heart surgery and during the surgery I had total heart block failure. The cardiologist hooked up an external pacemaker to the outside of my body. For 3 weeks I waited to see if my own heart would kick in. It never did. On the Friday that I was to have a pacemaker implanted internally, I accidentally pulled the wires leading from my external pacemaker to my heart when I hugged someone. Due to my situation, my heart was beating only about 10-17 beats per minute on its own. My doctor informed me that they would have to be very lenient with the anesthesia. If given too much anesthesia, I would die.

I remember feeling this excruciating, hot jot of electricity shoot through my entire being and then I heard my doctor say, "It's not going through. We're going to have to try it again."

He was trying to lead the pacemaker wires form the box through my veins into my heart.

I thought, "Oh, my God, they're doing surgery and I'm awake."

First I tried to open my eyes. I couldn't. They were taped shut. Then the doctor tried getting the wire through once more and I again felt that excruciating jolt of electricity shoot through my body. At this point I tried to scream, but the oxygen tube was crammed down my throat. I was nearing a panic. I tried moving my hands, my arms, but they were taped or restrained to the side of the cold, metal steel table.

Again my doctor said, "Let's try it one more time!"

I wanted to die. I braced myself for the jolt of electricity that was about to engage through my body for a third time. As soon as the hot, steel-like pain ceased to exist, I tried moving my toes.

Finally, I heard someone say, "Give her more gas, she's coming to." Once again, I faded away...only to come to once more, while the doctor was stitching up the pacemaker location sight. I could feel the needle prick my skin and the yank of the needle as the two sides of flesh came together as one. During this round, I endured less pain, because they quickly realized I was waking up.

Unlike the people on "Inside Edition", I did not feel jilted or angry in any way. My doctor clearly informed me of the dangers before the surgery ever began.

I do feel that all patients should be informed of the possibility of coming to during surgery. Perhaps patients should be required to sign a consent form stating that they understand the possibility of awareness occurring.

In the long run, I think most people would choose the possibility of awakening during a surgery as opposed to death. I would!

(name withheld)
Dallas, Texas

Awareness,

Until I saw the January 26, 1995 program on "Inside Edition," I did not know that so many others had experienced "awareness" during surgery. I thought mine was an isolated incident and never really discussed it with anyone except my wife and family. However, I did tell the doctors at the time and they acted very skeptical that I had actually undergone such an experience. They never entered it in my medical files. One doctor did act as if he may have believed me.

On August 17, 1991 I was scheduled for exploratory surgery at the Veterans' Administration Medical Center. I had been admitted three days before suffering from severe pain in my upper right abdomen. The doctors thought I had gall bladder trouble, gall stones or liver problems. However, a sonogram showed a hazy area in the appendix region, but unusually high in the abdomen. About 5:15 p.m. I was wheeled into surgery and given a shot to relax me. When the anesthetic was started through the IV in my arm, I could not seem to catch my breath, but I went under during the gasping and was under for I don't know how long. Suddenly I became alert and was feeling the worst pain I have ever felt in my life. I was being cut on and stretchers had been inserted in the incision and it felt as though I had a fire burning in my belly and I could feel the tissue ripping and stretching. I later found that the incision was started at my navel and extended down about 8" to my lower abdomen. My appendix had burst earlier, but had sealed itself up and was growing to the lining of my abdomen. It was removed successfully, but I was alert to what was going on and unable to do anything about it. I could not move anything to alert anyone and could not utter a sound, as I was completely paralyzed and unable to move. I remember thinking that my weak heart would probably give out from the pain if no one noticed my distress. I found I could only lie there and pray that someone would notice my condition. I could hear doctors calling for instruments and did hear someone say, "There's something wrong here."

I don't know if they were referring to my appendix or if someone may have noticed a change in heart rate or blood pressure on the monitors. I do not know how long I was awake, but hospital records indicate that the operation lasted about 2 hours altogether. I remember coming to again in ICU and telling my wife, "I was awake during that damned operation."

I told the nurse in ICU and she had a doctor come and talk to me. He did not seem too concerned until I described to him how helpless I felt from being paralyzed and how I could hear conversations during the procedure. He said that he believed that I probably was awake during part of it, but it was probably due to light as possible anesthetic being administered due to my heart condition. I told him that I thought the pain would probably have killed me quicker than a heavier dose of anesthetic.

I was discharged in 11 days and got along fine, but I now know how it feels to be skinned alive and would be very reluctant to undergo any surgery again.

"Inside Edition" gave this address, so I thought I'd share my experience with you, so that maybe this type of problem will be addressed by the medical profession and some type of monitors can be used to tell the doctors when this type of incident is occurring. Apparently it happens more often than we have been led to believe.

Anyway, I hope this letter may result in more precautions being taken to save others from this very, very painful experience.

Thank you.
(name withheld)
Gallatin, Missouri

Dear Sir/Madam:

I saw the February 4 Inside Edition segment about awareness during surgery on Channel 4 in Washington, DC.

I had gallbladder surgery in 1986. I "woke up" apparently near the end of the surgery. I attempted to open my eyes or move, but was unable to do either. I felt no pain, but did feel pressure in my abdominal area. I also felt the tube going down my throat and felt like I couldn't breathe.

I also heard the doctor talking to the nurses and assistant. When it was time to close, the doctor started singing "Rocky Top Tennessee."

I don't think anyone believed me until I told the anesthesiologist that I heard the surgeon singing. After he heard that, he seemed shocked and became very concerned. He admitted that the doctor did indeed sing "Rocky Top" and that sometimes during the end of surgery they administer Ativan or another tranquilizer that is supposed to make the patient forget any such memories.

The comment about administering a tranquilizer to make sure the patient "forgets" such memories seemed unbelievable to me. I was later told the same thing by a neurosurgeon. That they would knowingly allow someone to go through this thinking that they could erase such memories seems unethical and irresponsible to me.

My concern now is that I will have to go into surgery again some day and experience this again. Will it help to let them know in advance that I had such an experience and that I do not want to go through such an experience again even if they can later make me forget?

I would appreciate any additional information about this problem and your association.

Sincerely,
(name withheld)
Memphis, Tennessee

Dear Sir or Madam:

I recently watched a television program, Inside Edition, about anesthesia not working during major surgery. I had this experience on April 9, 1973, nearly 22 years ago. I had been taken to _____ in Tucson for an emergency appendectomy for acute appendicitis. The surgery was performed by Dr. _____, assisted by _____, MD While on the operating table I was administered anesthesia by a doctor from _____, in Tucson.

The anesthesia was adequate to put me to sleep; however, it did not keep me asleep. At some point during surgery I woke up with excruciating pain in my abdominal area. I could feel pressure against my abdomen. I thought they were in the process of sewing me up. I could hear the doctors carrying on casual conversations with one another. At one point, one doctor was talking about a pleasure trip he had taken to Mexico. The pain was so bad! I thought they would administer more anesthesia, but they didn't. I tried to move or to say something, a grunt, anything, but I was paralyzed. No sound would come out; nothing would move. Finally I could feel perspiration on my forehead! Apparently they saw that and administered more anesthesia, for I soon fell asleep again and experienced no more pain until I arrived in the recovery room. At that point I was wide awake and again in excruciating pain. I begged the nurses for a pain killer but, of course, they ignored my pleas.

That was my experience with awareness during surgery. I had never heard of such a thing prior to my surgery and until I saw that program on Inside Edition.

I hope my experience might in some way help in the research of the subject matter.

Sincerely,
(name withheld)
Tucson, Arizona

To Whom It May Concern,

I was pleased to hear the tail end of your segment on television. I hope I got enough of the address to get this to you as I was not prepared to be writing it down and had to rely on memory.

I would love to receive any information you have on this awareness during surgery. I had this experience on December 1977, while having a C-section birth with my daughter. At the time, I told my specialist (afterwards) that I had been awake for the section. He said no, I was just dreaming. I then told him several poignant facts and he looked very surprised, to say the least. He then said the anesthetist would talk to me. I told him the story and that is the last of it.

To date, I don't know why this happened. I have thought of seeing if it was on my medical records, but am not sure they would still have my records after 17 years. I do remember trying to get their attention during surgery by my heartbeat or blood pressure raising, and would love to know if I did raise it and was it ignored, or was there no change in these, even though I was frantic!

I hope to hear from you.
Sincerely,
(name withheld)
British Columbia, Canada

REFERENCES

1. Foreman J. This Is No Time to Wake Up, But Many Do. *Boston Globe.* May 1, 1995:29.

2. Willwerth J. What's Up Doc? *Time.* November 3, 1997:96.

3. Marcus MB. Waking Up Under the Surgeon's Knife. *U.S. News & World Report.* October 12, 1998:7.

CHAPTER 10

HEALING
"You have the answers within you."

I t was shortly after my *Dateline* interview in 1996 that I began to wonder just how far I should go to help others through their struggle with awareness. Then a very simple thought occurred to me. I could pray for them. So I made a promise to myself and to God after that show. I vowed that anytime I was blessed with the opportunity to share my message in an interview, I would spend the next day praying for the world. It may be corny, but that's me. So for nine hours, I would pray and give thanks for the world. My faith, which was already strong, went off into new dimensions. It became huge. The strength that came from it helped me to focus and have the drive to achieve every-thing on my plate. I felt healthy, my nightmares vanished, and good mem-ories were returning.

Trust yourself, you have the answers within you. Believe in yourself and believe that you are in control. You may have lost control for a time— on the operating table— but now you have regained it.

I decided to become an ordained minister. I made the decision to study all religions, so that whoever I might speak with, I would be able to speak with them on a spiritual level consistent with their own beliefs and thoughts, and with respect. I began to contact seminaries. It seemed that everywhere I turned, a door would close. I wondered why. I was trying to do good. I was trying to heal broken lives, not only with education and knowledge, but with spiritual tools as well. We all have needs that go beyond our material lives.

I finally found a seminary that allowed me to present my reason for wanting to attend. A lot of people told me I was biting off more than I could chew—that one religion was enough, let alone all of them. But it was something I knew I needed to do and it didn't matter if anyone else understood that. So I began my spiritual journey.

As a result of everything I have learned from my experiences, my conversations with others, and my commitment to AWARE, there is one prevailing thought that applies to everyone who has experienced awareness or some other trauma in their lives: All of us have our own individual needs. The best thing we can do is to ask ourselves this question: "What do I need in order to heal?"

I encourage you to write down your answers. We usually have all we need within ourselves. We often give up that power, thinking that because of the situation we are dealing with at the time our judgment is clouded. Often people will seek answers elsewhere and find only confusion. Trust yourself, you have the answers within you. Believe in yourself and believe

140

that you are in control. You may have lost control for a time—on the operating table—but now you have regained it.

The best solution I have found for establishing control is meditation and prayer. Some people find it helps to take a walk in the morning, the evening, or during lunch time. Running, swimming, and yoga are also effective methods for dealing with stress.

Whatever you can do to get rid of stress from your mind and body will bring balance into your life. Establish a regular routine and stick with it. It takes 21 days to break a habit. Each and every day you'll begin to look more and more forward to your task.

Your life will become easier to handle on all levels when you begin to find ways to replace the pain. A tremendous sense of peace will come over you, whether you're at home or at the office. I highly recommend finding what it is that works for you.

Now let me share some of the things that don't help. Crowded places, for instance, can create problems. Often, people who have experienced awareness tend to feel claustrophobic. Malls, stores, and noisy places can be overwhelming. Taking on more than you can handle should be avoided. For one thing, it usually means rushing, but it also takes away from your own personal quiet time.

Be careful of overeating, drinking, and smoking. You will be upset with yourself for doing so. You should also avoid a closed environment without light. If you have an office without a window, you might want to use an environmental lamp. Try listening to soft, tranquil music to keep you calm and relaxed. Don't let yourself become overtired or exhausted. Don't worry about what people are thinking or what they'll say. Take care of yourself. You're in the healing process. Get your proper sleep and eat three meals a day, especially breakfast—even if it's just a piece of toast. Have something healthy at lunch. And at dinner, eat a little less—it's harder to sleep at night

I say an affirmation each night before I fall asleep. I tell myself, "I am safe, I am strong, I am healthy, everything is perfect in its own way and God is with me." And I repeat the words over and over until I fall asleep.

otherwise. Walk after dinner, or take a warm bath. Unwind before bed—try reading a soothing, positive book (murder mysteries don't count). A book of affirmations can be very uplifting. There are many books that can help in the healing process.

I say an affirmation each night before I fall asleep. I tell myself, "I am safe, I am strong, I am healthy, everything is perfect in its own way and God is with me." And I repeat the words over and over until I fall asleep.

You can even do affirmations when you're driving. Rush hour traffic was difficult for me for years. I remember one time leaving my car in the middle of rush hour in Washington, D.C. I parked the car in the fast lane and tried to get to the side of the road and catch my breath because I was feeling claustrophobic in my car. The traffic was intense, and I felt like I couldn't breathe.

You will discover for yourself the difficulties with which you will have to deal. Some people only have one or two, some have many more. Either way, all that matters is what *you* are personally experiencing. Come back to center and love yourself. If you don't feel that you can handle something, don't be afraid to say no. If you feel like crying, then cry. If you're tired and not sleeping at night, if you're not eating because your stomach is in knots, take care of yourself. Be gentle and accept your emotions as they arrive. If you are hard on yourself or try to force yourself to stop feeling a certain way, you'll just drag it out longer. So as the waves of emotions come, accept them and tell yourself, "This too shall pass."

You are your best teacher, mentor and feeling detector. This is because you know what makes you feel good and what doesn't. Common sense will be your guide. It's about you. Don't worry what anyone else has to say. Look at how strong you are.

Don't be afraid to answer the question, "What would make me feel better?" Whatever it is, it rebuilds the energy within you to go on another day or another hour or another five minutes. You have it already. By finding your power within, you will find a stronger person than you ever knew existed within you. We all like to think we are strong, but you only know the limits of your strength when it is tested. After surviving my ordeal on the operating table, I now know that whatever obstacle comes my way, I'll be able to overcome it. You have to be able to take a negative and turn it into something positive. It's up to you. It's your life. I chose to fight it because I wasn't about to lose my life. It was not my fault what had happened. I could have continued to blame those who had erred, but I would have remained stuck in that situation. It was just as painful dealing with the aftermath. I had to choose where I wanted to take my life.

It's human nature to cast blame when you're injured in some way. But it's your choice how long you want to continue casting blame. There was an affirmation I used when it came to choices. I would say, "Every choice I make today will be the right choice for me."

Healing is about you—not anyone else. You

If you are hard on yourself or try to force yourself to stop feeling a certain way, you'll just drag it out longer. So as the waves of emotions come, accept them and tell yourself, "This too shall pass."

Healing is about you—not anyone else. You make the time and you take the time to do what is necessary for you.

143

> *Sometimes it is through pain, loneliness, confusion and fear that we gain our strength, power, wisdom and courage.*

make the time and you take the time to do what is necessary for you. As I went through therapy, I learned a great deal about myself in the process. I was not going to be ashamed that I had experienced surgical awareness and my life had changed. I wasn't going to be embarrassed that I had to take time each week to talk to someone about it. I can remember sitting in my therapy sessions and grabbing the box of tissues and crying for a whole hour. Then I would get up and thank my therapist for just letting me be. It was a safe place where I could talk if I wanted to, but I didn't have to talk at all if I preferred. When you find a therapist that gives you that freedom, you heal faster. You learn to make rational decisions instead of impulsive ones out of fear and misunderstanding. Everyone is different. You may need a few weeks of therapy, or a few years. What matters is that you get what you need.

There were times when I couldn't wait seven days until my next appointment. I would be in there two or three times a week and I didn't care what anyone thought or had to say about it. They didn't have a clue what I was going through. The only person I could depend on to take care of me was *me.*

When you come into alignment with yourself you can trust yourself. Take time for yourself, be proud of yourself, and know that everything is going to be fine. You'll have bad days, you'll have lonely days, you'll have fearful days—the good news is that you're still here to have them.

I would often ask myself when something was bothering me, "Will this matter a few days from now?" It allowed me to put things into perspective. It is perspective that allows me to share what I know about the pain associated with awareness. I know because I have been through it myself. I also know it can turn out all right.

144

What an adventure we have been offered in life. Sometimes it is through pain, loneliness, confusion and fear that we gain our strength, power, wisdom and courage. Hard times allow us to discover what's important. Isn't that the ultimate question? What is important in your life? Is it fame? Fortune? Power? For me it is simply life itself.

There's a reason why I went through my ordeal; there's a reason why anyone does. Imagine if we as patients and those administering anesthesia in the operating room can come together to bring anesthetic awareness out into the light of day. I see it happening. I know that for sure my own speaking out has already educated many and brought about needed changes.

For those who don't think that awareness is a real problem, it may take an experience on the operating table. There are those who won't understand until it happens to them. That strikes me as sad. Why is it that change cannot come easily and take place quickly? Why does a catastrophe have to be the catalyst? If I had died nobody would have known what really had happened to me; I had to live to let people know about awareness.

If we as survivors of awareness are going to make a difference, the first thing we have to do is heal ourselves. The next step is to ask what we can do to bring about change. Finally, be thankful the incident occurred. Now that might sound crazy. I know that if anyone had come to me years ago and told me to be "thankful" for my anesthetic awareness experience, I would have thought they were insane. I would have become angry and defensive. But I can tell you today that I thank God for every single minute because it has helped me to become the person I am today. Give thanks. Touch a life.

CHAPTER 11

ANESTHESIA IN THE 21ST CENTURY
A Journey of Progress

by Sandra M. Ouellette, CRNA, MEd, FAAN, and
Richard G. Ouellette, CRNA, MEd

odern surgical anesthesia had its beginning
in the 1800s when dentists and other physi-
cians sought remedies to provide pain-free
surgical procedures. In those days, surgery was undertaken only in extreme
circumstances and the mark of a good surgeon was how fast the procedure
could be accomplished. Developments in anesthesia over the last 160 years
have removed patient fear of a painful experience and allowed unprecented
advances in surgical interventions. This area of therapeutic intervention has
progressed from the painful appendectomies, amputations, and Cesarean
sections of the 1800s to pain-free cardiac, neurological, and transplant surgery today. Today, the induction and maintenance of anesthesia is a com-

147

plex process that has become highly refined. Safety is the primary goal in managing of the anesthetized patient.

The purpose of this chapter is to acquaint the reader with progress made in anesthesia from its beginning until now. Anesthesia is defined, major providers of anesthesia identified, and factors associated with anesthesia discussed. Other topics covered include: types of anesthesia available to patients; standards of anesthesia practice and process; potential complications that may be associated with anesthesia; and the patient's role in improving safety during anesthesia.

THE HISTORY OF ANESTHESIA

Prior to 1846, surgical procedures were uncommon. Surgical techniques were poorly developed, infections associated with surgery were common, and anesthesia was unavailable. When surgery had to be done, alcohol, hashish, or opium derivatives were used in an attempt to dull the patient's senses. Physical methods such as packing an extremity in ice, making the extremity ischemic and numb, or a physical blow to the head to produce unconsciousness, were also used. At times, several strong men would physically restrain the patient until the procedure was completed.

As early as 1842, ether was used to produce surgical anesthesia (Table 1). In 1844, nitrous oxide, an agent synthesized in 1776, was used to produce dental analgesia (the inability to feel pain while conscious). Public demonstrations of intoxication from ether and nitrous oxide were common in the 1800s. During one demonstration, Dr. Horace Wells, a dentist, noted that a patient was injured under the influence of nitrous oxide but felt no pain. Dr. Wells later had painless dental extractions himself and in 1845 attempted to demonstrate this miracle. Unfortunately, the patient cried out during the demonstration and Wells was labeled a fraud and failure.

TABLE 1. HISTORY OF ANESTHESIA

1776	Nitrous oxide synthesized by Priestly
1842	Diethyl ether used by Long to produce surgical analgesia
1845	Nitrous oxide used by Wells to produce dental analgesia
1846	Diethyl ether used publically by Morton to produce anesthesia
1847	Chloroform used for surgical anesthesia in England
1847	Simpson administered ether to a patient to relieve pain of labor
1853	Chloroform administered by Snow to Queen Victoria for the birth of Prince Leopold
1854	Hollow metallic needle invented by Wood
1884	Cocaine used by Koller to produce topical anesthesia
1885	Nerve block and infiltration anesthesia by injection of cocaine introduced by Halsted; epidural anesthesia introduced by Corning
1898	Spinal anesthesia introduced by Bier
1905	Procaine synthesized by Einhorn
1917	Oxygen mask developed by Poulton
1920	Guedel published data on signs of ether anesthesia; tracheal tubes for delivery of inhaled anesthetics introduced by Magill
1930	Circle anesthetic breathing and carbon dioxide absorption system described by Sword
1933	Cyclopropane used by Waters to produce surgical anesthesia
1934	Thiopental used by Lundy for induction of anesthesia
1942	d-tubocurarine used by Griffith and Johnson to produce muscle relaxation during general anesthesia
1943	Lidocaine synthesized by Lofgren

(continued)

1949	Succinylcholine used clinically by Phillips, Fusco for muscle relaxation
1954	Fluroxene introduced clinically (inhaled agent)
1956	Halothane used clinically by Johnson (inhaled agent)
1959	Methoxyflurane used clinically by Artusio and Von Pozaak (inhaled agent)
1972	Enflurane used clinically (inhaled agent)
1981	Isoflurane used clinically (inhaled agent)
1989	Propofol used clinically
1992	Desflurane used clinically (inhaled agent)
1994	Sevoflurane used clinically (inhaled agent); Rocuronium, muscle relaxant
1996	Cisatracurium, muscle relaxant

Dr. Crawford Long, a practitioner from Georgia, was the first physician known to administer ether; however, his work was not published. As a result, Dr. William Morton, a dentist, became the first recognized "anesthetist," when he received public recognition for successful anesthesia in 1846. Morton's demonstration occurred in "the ether dome" at Massachusetts General Hospital. The oft-repeated story goes like this:

"In the gallery of this room skeptical spectators gathered for the news and spread that a second-year medical student had developed a method for abolishing surgical pain. The patient, Gilbert Abbott, was brought in and Dr. Warren, the surgeon, waited in formal morning clothes. Operating gowns, masks, gloves, surgical asepsis, and the bacterial origin of infection were entirely unknown at that time. Everyone was ready and waiting, including the strong men to hold down the struggling patient, but Morton did not appear.

Fifteen minutes passed and the surgeon, becoming impatient, took his scalpel, turned to the gallery, and said, 'As Dr. Moron has not arrived, I presume he is otherwise engaged.' While the audience smiled and the patient cringed, the surgeon turned to make his incision. Just then Morton entered, his tardiness being due to the necessity for completing an apparatus with which to administer ether. Warren stepped back and, pointing to the man strapped to the operating table, said, 'Well, sir, your patient is ready.' Surrounded by a silent and unsympathetic audience, Morton went quietly to work. After a few minutes of ether inhalation, the patient was unconscious, whereupon Morton looked up and said, 'Dr. Warren, your patient is ready." The operation was begun. The patient showed no sign of pain, yet he was alive and breathing. The strong men were not needed. When the operation was completed, Dr. Warren turned to the astonished audience and made the famous statement, 'Gentlemen, this is no humbug.' Dr. Henry J. Bigelow, an eminent surgeon attending the demonstration, remarked, 'I have seen something today that will go around the world.' "[1]

This wonderful news quickly spread throughout the world. A monument erected over the grave of Dr. Morton in Mt. Auburn Cemetery near Boston honors the man given credit for the introduction of surgical anesthesia with an inscription that reads:

WILLIAM T. G. MORTON

Inventor and Revealer of Anaesthetic Inhalation.

Before Whom, in all Time, Surgery Was Agony.

By Whom Pain in Surgery Was Averted and Annulled.

Since Whom Science Has Control of Pain.[1]

While the introduction of surgical anesthesia was an American contribution, the use of anesthesia to relieve pain during childbirth came from England. In 1847, Dr. James Simpson, an obstetrician, administered ether to a pregnant patient to relieve her pains. Six years later, the use of chloroform for obstetric anesthesia became accepted by the public when Dr. John Snow administered the drug to Queen Victoria during the birth of Prince Leopold.[2]

Anesthesia in the 1800s consisted of the use of agents such as nitrous oxide, ether, chloroform, and cocaine for topical anesthesia. During the later part of that century, spinal anesthesia was introduced and patients were able to undergo pain-free surgical procedures while remaining conscious. In 1934, sodium pentothal, the first intravenous drug, was introduced to produce unconsciousness. Use of sodium pentothal was followed in 1942 with the introduction of d-tubocurarine, the first drug used clinically to produce skeletal muscle relaxation. By now it was possible to produce a controlled, reversible pharmacological coma that allowed patients to have surgical or diagnostic procedures without pain.

During the next 60 years, marked improvements were made in the field of anesthesia. Multiple agents, each better than the last, were introduced. The site of pharmacological action became more specific and the agents more reliable in controllability by the anesthesia provider. Tremendous improvements were made in monitoring technology and in the education of physicians and nurses who specialized in anesthesia. While a shortage exists today in anesthesia providers, there is no shortage of surgical or diagnostic procedures, many of which require the use of anesthesia. In 1998, 41.5 million inpatient procedures were performed in nonfederal, short-stay hospitals; and in 1996, 31.5 million surgical procedures were performed on outpatients in nonfederal hospitals and free-standing ambulatory surgery centers.[3] These figures do not include procedures performed in dentist, podiatrist, and physicians' offices.

What is Anesthesia?

The term anesthesia is derived from the Greek word *"anaisthesia,"* which means insensibility. It is a term denoting loss of sensation with or without loss of consciousness. The practice of anesthesia is a recognized specialty in both nursing and medicine. The nurse specialist is referred to as a Certified Registered Nurse Anesthetist (CRNA), and the physician is called an anesthesiologist in the United States and anaesthetist in most other parts of the world.

The target site for most anesthetic drugs is the central nervous system (CNS). The anesthetic state can be produced by sedatives, local anesthetics applied to nerves, or agents that have a global or site-specific depressant effect within the nervous system. General anesthetics produce a reversible, irregular, descending depression of the CNS leading to unconsciousness. This generalized state of nervous system depression and unconsciousness may be produced by one drug or several drugs in combination. One drug may provide hypnosis or unconsciousness, another analgesia, another amnesia, and yet another muscle relaxation. They complement each other in producing the anesthetized state.

Global agents have widespread effects throughout the CNS or brain and spinal cord. In contrast, sitespecific agents produce their pharmacological effects by interaction with specific receptors in the central or peripheral nervous system (Table 2). Nitrous oxide and volatile or inhaled agents (halothane, isoflurane, desflurane, sevoflurane, nitrous oxide) and intravenous hypnotics (propofol, thiopental) lead to unconsciousness. They have a generalized effect on the brain. In contrast, opioids (morphine, fentanyl) exert their effect by interaction with opioid receptors in the brain and spinal cord. Benzodiazepines (valium, midazolam) interact with benzodiazopine receptors to produce sedation, amnesia, reduced levels of anxiety, and muscle relaxation. Muscle relaxants (d-tubocurarine, succinylcholine, rocuronium, etc.) do not alter the state of consciousness but do provide skeletal muscle relaxation.

153

TABLE 2. COMPONENTS OF ANESTHESIA

	Hypnosis	Analgesia	Amnesia	Relaxation
Global Agents				
Volatile agents	+++	+/-	+	+
Propofol I	+++	-	+	+/-
Thiopental	+++	+	+	o
Nitrous oxide	+		+	o
Site-specific Agents				
Opioids	+/-	+++	o	-
Benzodiazepines	+	o	+++	o
Muscle relaxants	o	o	o	+++

+++	= primary effect
+	= weaker effect
+/-	= doubtful effect
o	= no effect
-	= antagonist effect

In general, agents that produce their effect by interaction with specific receptors can be reversed. Drugs that interact with a receptor and produce a pharmacologic effect are called agonist; drugs that interact with a receptor and prevent or reverse the pharmacological effect are known as antagonist. For example, morphine is an opioid agonist and naloxone an opioid antagonist. Reversibility is an advantage associated with many site-specific drugs used in anesthesia.

Agents capable of producing anesthesia may be administered by inhalation, intramuscular or intravenous injection, or by administration through the gastrointestinal tract. A balanced anesthetic technique consists of the use of several drugs, each of which addresses one or more of the four components of anesthesia. Light general anesthesia implies an anesthetic state with minimal depression of physiologic functions and at a level from which the patient returns to the conscious state quickly. Deep general anesthesia implies a state of physiological depression just short of undesired side effects, which may require intervention to support respiration, blood pressure, etc. Light versus deep general anesthesia is on a continuum that quickly and constantly changes according to levels of surgical stress and the amount of anesthetic given. Anesthetic depth during general anesthesia is assessed through sensory, motor, and autonomic responses controlled by the voluntary and involuntary nervous system. Depth of anesthesia is an inexact term referring to the progressive attenuation of the patient's response to painful stimuli as increasing quantities of anesthesia are administered.

Types of Anesthesia

There are three types of anesthesia: local, regional, and general. With *local anesthesia*, an agent that anesthetizes nerves is injected into a site near where the procedure will be done. For example. a dentist will administer a local anesthetic before dental extraction. At times, an anesthesia specialist such as a CRNA or anesthesiologist will care for the patients and provide sedation during the local anesthesia. When this occurs, the term monitored anesthesia care is used. Whether the technique involves only local or local agents combined with sedatives, during this type of anesthetic patients are awake or in a light sleep from which they are easily aroused. This type of anesthesia may also be called conscious sedation. Patients receiving conscious sedation are usually able to speak and respond to verbal commands throughout the procedure. A brief period of amnesia may erase any memory of the procedure, however.

Regional anesthesia involves the injection of a local anesthetic agent near a nerve to diminish or eliminate sensory and motor function. A main advantage of this technique is the ability to anesthetize an area of the body to

155

prevent pain during a diagnostic or surgical procedure without the system-wide effects associated with general anesthesia. This technique may include an upper extremity block or production of anesthesia by injection of an agent into the subarachnoid or epidural space. A subarachnoid injection is called a spinal anesthetic and is most commonly used for surgical procedures involving the lower abdomen or lower extremities. An epidural anesthetic is used to provide anesthesia to a specific area of the body and also is used to provide postoperative analgesia. Epidural anesthesia is a popular technique for labor and delivery. An advantage in this situation is that it allows most women to participate fully in the birth experience while relieving most, if not all, labor pains. Table 3 compares several different anesthesia techniques.

When local anesthesia techniques are used, patients are generally awake. They may feel touch or pressure, but not pain. They may hear conversations and will be able to follow commands. At times intravenous sedatives will be used to produce sleep or amnesia.

General anesthesia is administered by giving anesthetic drugs intravenously and/or having patients breathe anesthetic gases. Patients are unconscious. The choice between local, regional, or general anesthesia depends on the complexity of the procedure, the surgeon, and patient preference. The selection of anesthetic agents depends on the technique chosen (local, regional, or general), the length of the procedure, side effects associated with the use of each drug, patient age and physical status, and the preferences of both the patient and anesthesia provider.[4]

THE ANESTHETIC PROCESS: STANDARDS OF PRACTICE

A good way to describe the anesthetic process to those unfamiliar with anesthesia is to address standards of practice. Standards are published, authorative statements that describe a practitioner's responsibilities for orga-

156

nizational membership and principles of practice. Most professional organizations have adopted standards. Table 4 identifies standards for nurse anesthesia practice: These are descriptive of what patients might expect from their CRNA during the perioperative period, and assist CRNAs in providing constant, safe anesthesia care.[5]

TABLE 3. ANESTHETIC TECHNIQUES	
Technique	**Definition**
Conscious Sedation	An altered state of consciousness that minimizes pain and discomfort through the use of pain relievers and sedatives
Monitored Anesthesia Care	Local anesthesia or local anesthesia with sedation by an anesthetist
Regional Anesthesia	
• Pudendal Block	Injection of local anesthetic, which numbs the vaginal area; often used for delivery
• Spinal Anesthesia	Injection of local anesthetics into the spinal canal to relieve pain
• Epidural Anesthesia	Method of delivering pain-relief drugs through a tiny tube called a catheter placed in the back outside the spinal cord; may be used for anesthesia or analgesia postoperatively
General Anesthesia	Administration of drugs intramuscularly, intravenously, or through inhalation, which cause unconsciousness

Standard I	A thorough and complete preanesthetic assessment shall be performed.
Standard II	Informed consent for the planned anesthetic intervention shall be obtained from the patient or legal guardian.
Standard III	A patient-specific plan of anesthesia care shall be formulated.
Standard IV	The anesthesia care plan shall be skillfully implemented and the plan of care adjusted as needed to adapt to the patient's response to the anesthetic. Vigilance shall be maintained for untoward identifiable reactions and corrective actions initiated as required.
Standard V	The patient's physiologic condition shall be monitored consistent with both the type of anesthesia care and specific patient needs.
Standard VI	There shall be prompt, complete, and accurate documentation of pertinent information on the patient's record.
Standard VII	The responsibility for the care of the patient shall be transferred to other qualified providers in a manner that assures continuity of care and patient safety.
Standard VIII	Appropriate safety precautions shall be taken to minimize the risk of fire, explosions, electrical shock, and equipment malfunction.
Standard IX	Appropriate safety precautions shall be taken to minimize the risk of infection for the patient, CRNA, and other staff.

(continued)

Standard X	Anesthesia care shall be assessed to assure its quality.
Standard XI	The CRNA shall respect and maintain the basic rights of patients, demonstrating concern for personal dignity and human relationships.

In order to develop an anesthetic plan that is patient specific, a pre-anesthetic assessment is necessary. Components of the assessment include relevant history, physical examination, medication history, and laboratory studies. Table 5 identifies information generally obtained during the history. Thoughtful responses to these questions by the patient help the anesthesia provider develop a management plan.

The physical examination provides other information pertinent to anesthesia and may identify areas associated with possible complications. The head and neck are assessed for neck flexion, mouth opening, and dentition. Veins are evaluated for access and skin color is noted. The presence or absence of peripheral edema, bruising, or petechiae is noted as well. Auscultation of the heart and lungs is done and normal blood pressure noted. Laboratory tests are requested when the history or physical suggests that a condition exists which may have an effect on anesthetic or surgical outcome.

Once the patient is evaluated, the anesthetic plan is discussed. In addition to the planned approach, alternative techniques are described if appropriate. Potential risks are highlighted and the patient then signs an anesthetic informed consent statement. This statement generally includes rare but possible complications associated with administration of anesthesia. Potential complications noted on many disclosure forms are discussed at the close of this chapter.

TABLE 5. PREANESTHETIC QUESTIONS

Do you have or have you had:

- Allergies to medications?

- A recent cold or flu?

- Chest pain (angina)?

- Heart condition?

- Heart attack (myocardial infarction)?

- High blood pressure?

- Shortness of breath?

- Asthma, bronchitis, or any other breathing problem?

- Heart catheterization?

- Heart surgery?

- Irregular heart beats?

- Pacemaker?

- Automatic defibrillator?

- Sugar diabetes?

- Hepatitis, liver disease, jaundice?

- A thyroid condition?

- Kidney disease?

- Cancer?

- Chemotherapy?

- Radiation therapy?

- Hemophilia?

- Bleeding diseases?

- Anemia?

- Muscle disease?   *(continued)*

- Tuberculosis?

- Seizures?

- Passing out spells?

- Stroke?

- Ulcers or other stomach condition?

- Hiatal hernia?

- Numbness, weakness, paralysis of extremities?

Do you:
- Smoke? _____ Packs/day? _____ Number of years?

- Drink alcohol? _____ Drinks/week?

- Take or have you taken recreational drugs?

- Take herbal medications (Such as St. John's Wort)?

- Take or have you taken cortisone (steroids) in the last six months?

- Take any nonsteroidal, anti-inflammatory drugs?

- Have loose, chipped, or false teeth? Bridgework? Oral piercings?

- Wear contact lens?

Have you or a family member had:
- Malignant hyperthermia?

- Sickle cell disease?

- Hemophilia?

- Complications after surgery?

Have you:
- Donated blood for surgery?

- Had nausea and vomiting after surgery?

- Are you pregnant? _____Due date?

Following careful evaluation of all pertinent factors discovered in the preanesthetic assessment, a plan of care is developed by the anesthesia provider in coordination with other appropriate healthcare providers. The plan is based on assessment, analysis of information provided by the patient, the anticipated procedure including its length and complexity, patient preference, and current anesthesia principles. The plan may vary even for the same procedure depending on the elective or emergent nature of the surgery and physical condition of the patient.

An anesthesia provider, usually a CRNA, is in constant attendance throughout the operative procedure. In addition to maintaining appropriate levels of anesthesia, this provider is responsible for patient safety. Continuous monitoring (outlined in Table 6) is of critical importance.[6] From the time the anesthesia provider's constant attendance begins until the care of the patient is turned over to qualified professionals in the postanesthesia care unit or intensive care unit, the patient is monitored. The degree of monitoring is consistent with both the type of anesthesia care and the specific patient's needs. Continuous clinical observation and vigilance by the anesthesia provider are the basis of safe anesthesia care.

During the procedure, the anesthesia provider promptly, completely, and accurately documents pertinent information on the patient's record. Such documentation includes all anesthetic interventions and patient responses. Accurate recording facilitates comprehensive patient care, provides information for retrospective review and research, and establishes a medical-legal record should there be questions about the quality of care given.

At the end of the procedure, the anesthesia provider transfers care to other qualified healthcare professionals. Continuity of care is assured, and the anesthesia provider accurately reports the patient's condition and all essential information to personnel assuming responsibility for the care of the patient.

TABLE 6. MONITORING STANDARDS: AMERICAN ASSOCIATION OF NURSE ANESTHETISTS

A. Monitor ventilation continuously. Verify intubation of the trachea by auscultation, chest excursion, and confirmation of carbon dioxide in the expired gas. Continuously monitor end-tidal carbon dioxide during controlled or assisted ventilation. Use spirometry and ventilatory pressure monitors.

B. Monitor oxygenation continuously by clinical observation, pulse oximetry, and if indicated, arterial blood gas analysis.

C. Monitor cardiovascular status continuously via electrocardiogram and heart sounds. Record blood pressure and heart rate at least every five minutes.

D. Monitor body temperature continuously on all pediatric patients receiving general anesthesia and when indicated, on all other patients.

E. Monitor neuromuscular function and status when neuromuscular blocking agents are administered.

F. Monitor and assess the patient positioning and protective measures.

(Effective April 6, 1998.)

Throughout the anesthetic process, it is assured that equipment is functional and steps are taken to protect the patient from environmental risks such as fire, explosion, and electrical shock. Appropriate precautions are taken to minimize infection for the patient and staff. In other words, all attempts are made to ensure safety and make the experience pleasant for the patient.

COMPLICATIONS ASSOCIATED WITH ANESTHESIA

While most patients have uneventful anesthesia experiences, the administration of anesthesia is not an exact science. Complications can result from the use of any anesthetic. Potential complications are listed on Table 7.

TABLE 7. POTENTIAL ANESTHESIA COMPLICATIONS/RISKS

- Headache
- Back pain
- Brain damage
- Nerve injury
- Paralysis
- Damage to eyes, nose, skin
- Sore throat
- Dental damage
- Vocal cord injury
- Respiratory problems
- Windpipe injury
- Nausea and vomiting
- Damage to blood vessels
- Drug reactions
- Infection
- Esophageal laceration
- Heart damage
- Injury to baby if you are pregnant
- Awareness during general anesthesia
- Death

The administration of general anesthesia involves manipulation and instrumentation of the upper airway. Complications such as dental injury may occur, especially if teeth are loose or diseased, or if fixed dental work is in place. Dental injuries are one of the most common anesthesia-related malpractice claims reported, with an overall incidence ranging from 1:100

164

to 1:1,000 of all tracheal intubations performed in the United States.[7] Dental injuries are more common in children, in patients with periodontal disease where structural support is poor, or when patients have bridge work or capped teeth. Patients must notify their anesthesia provider of abnormal or diseased teeth or gums.

Trauma to the larynx is not uncommon after endotracheal intubation. It is usually minor and recovery is usually prompt with conservative treatment. Vocal cord paralysis, however, has occurred.[8] Paralysis may be unilateral or bilateral. Hoarseness is noted with unilateral paralysis while respiratory obstruction occurs with bilateral problems. Although permanent voice change has occurred, vocal cord paralysis associated with tracheal intubation is usually temporary. Essophageal laceration has also been reported. Fever or throat pain following a difficult intubation may mean perforation.

The incidence of sore throat after intubation is 40 percent, and may be as high as 65 percent when intubation is difficult.[9] The incidence is higher in women and in patients having thyroid surgery. Swallowing discomfort usually lasts no more than 24 to 48 hours and can be relieved by having the patient breathe humidified air.

Neurological complications range from headaches or back pain to brain death, which is greatly feared, but quite uncommon. Headaches are most often associated with spinal anesthesia and are referred to as postdural puncture headaches. They are thought to be due to the loss of cerebrospinal fluid through the dura or membrane that covers the spinal cord. Fluid loss places traction on intracranial vessels that respond with painful vasodilatation. The incidence is small, with a higher risk seen in young, ambulatory patients.

The 20 percent incidence of backache after surgery is similar to that found in the general population.[10] After anesthesia, transient backache occurs at an incidence of 30 percent following epidural anesthesia and 8 percent after general anesthesia."[11, 12] Backache after general anesthesia is usually mild and resolves in less than 48 hours. Therapy usually consists of mild analgesics.

The incidence of postoperative nausea and vomiting is approximately 30 percent.[13] This complication is seen more in children than adults and more in females than males. Patients with a history of motion sickness or postoperative nausea and vomiting after previous surgery are at greater risk. Anxiety and conditions such as diabetes mellitus with delayed gastric emptying also play a role in these unpleasant events.

Nausea and vomiting are more likely to occur after certain types of surgical procedures.[14] Gynecologic, general abdominal, head and neck surgery, pediatric, dental, laparoscopic, and some orthopedic procedures have greater risk. Pediatric patients having surgery of the head or neck are also at increased risk.[15] There are numerous pharmacologic and nonpharmacologic options available for prevention or treatment of postoperative nausea and vomiting, and management of this complication improves each year.

Drug reactions during anesthesia may vary from a minor rash to a major allergic reaction (anaphylaxis) with cardiovascular and respiratory compromise. Almost any drug can produce an anaphylactic reaction in the right patient and clinical manifestations generally involve the respiratory, cardiovascular, and cutaneous systems. Patients may experience a variety of symptoms, including: difficulty breathing, chest discomfort, coughing, wheezing, sneezing, dizziness, malaise, hypotension, hives, flushing, periorbital edema or perioral edema. Management of anaphylaxis includes oxygen, intravascular volume expansion, and epinephrine. Secondary treatments may include antihistamines, corticosteroids, and symptomatic therapy. Patients who have had anaphylactic reactions to drugs administered in the operating room require evaluation to identify the causal agents and to guide selection and use of future medications.[16]

The choice of anesthetic agents and techniques for the pregnant patient having nonobstetric surgery depends upon gestation and urgency of the procedure. It is estimated that 1 percent to 2 percent of pregnant women undergo anesthesia for surgical procedures unrelated to delivery each year.[17] Exposure of the fetus to drugs that could cause deformities is of concern in the first trimester, and risk of preterm delivery related to surgical stimulation or drugs is a concern in the third trimester. In spite of these concerns, over 75,000 pregnant patients a year have anesthesia or surgery without harm to the infant. If the procedure is elective, however, it should be postponed until after the baby is born. If the procedure is an emergency, it must be done. Regional anesthesia is used if possible, but general anesthesia is not inappropriate for well-monitored patients.

Although extremely rare in occurrence, awareness during general anesthesia does occur. The reported incidence of awareness during anesthesia depends on the type of anesthesia, strength of the stimulus, and the timing and persistence of attempts to elicit recall.[18] This potential complication will be addressed fully in the next chapter.

The most feared complication during anesthesia is permanent nerve injury or brain death. The reason for many intraoperative deaths is life-threatening injury or illness at the time of surgery in which there is little chance of survival. In extremely rare cases, serious patient harm occurs as a result of unexpected airway problems or respiratory or cardiovascular complications.

When assessing the risk of serious injury during anesthesia, all factors must be considered. Several decades ago, the risk of an adverse outcome associated with anesthesia was estimated to be 2:10,000 anesthetics. Today, studies conducted in Australia, the United Kingdom, and other countries indicate that anesthesia mortality rates are about 1 in 200,000 to 300,000 anesthetics administered.[19] Improved drugs, monitoring technologies, educational programs, and safety standards have resulted in safer passage from the anesthetized state to recovery. Vigilance of the anesthesia provider is also critically important.

Patient Contributions to the Desired Outcome

In the 21st century, patients expect comfort and an uncomplicated recovery from anesthesia. With the monitoring technologies and pharmacological agents available today, this goal is generally easily achieved. Patients, however, also contribute to satisfactory outcomes. The patient's role is in truthful, full participation in the areas listed in Table 8.

All recommendations made in Table 8 are important. For example, patients will generally be told to not ingest solid foods after midnight the night before surgery and avoid clear liquid within two to three hours of the scheduled procedure. This is to protect the lungs from gastric content once airway reflexes are depressed by the anesthetic. If the surgery is urgent and the patient has recently eaten, the anesthesia provider needs to know so special precautions can be taken to protect the lungs from aspiration.

Any drug a patient is taking, regardless of how minor it may seem, should be included in the list of medications the patient reveals to the anesthesia provider. Patients may tell their anesthesia provider about cardiac drugs they are taking, but may forget to disclose that they take aspirin and other over-the-counter, nonprescription drugs. Aspirin alters the coagulation system, in which case regional anesthesia might be avoided.

Approximately 15 million Americans have reported using herbs or high-dose vitamins and in a recent survey 22 percent of patients reported using herbal medications.[20] Women and adults between the ages of 40 to 60 are the most likely herbal consumers.[21] While many patients do not consider these herbal preparations to be "medications," they can indeed alter how the patient responds to anesthesia and surgery. For example, some herbal medications may increase anesthetic requirements, while others may increase bleeding or alter how patients will respond if a low blood pressure needs to be treated.[22] If in doubt, patients should inform their anesthesia provider about everything they are taking and let the professional decide what is important and what is not.

TABLE 8. PATIENT RESPONSIBILITY TOWARD A SAFE ANESTHETIC

1. Clearly answer questions from your anesthesia provider or other healthcare professional.

2. Follow instructions exactly.

3. Alert the anesthesia provider to any health conditions you might have.

4. Provide a list of medications or herbal preparations you are taking.

5. Be aware that recreational drugs, prescription drugs, and alcohol can affect anesthesia.

G. If you are pregnant, plan on anesthesia even if you intend to have natural childbirth.

7. Do not operate a car or heavy machinery for 24 hours after an anesthetic.

8. Do not take any drugs except those prescribed by your doctor following anesthesia.

9. Make sure you have a responsible adult to drive you home and stay with you after receiving an anesthetic.

REFERENCES

1. Kennedy SK, Longnecker DE. History and principles of anesthesiology. In: Gilman AG, Hardman JG, Limbird LE, eds. *The Pharmacological Basis of Therapeutics*. 9th ed. New York, NY: McGraw Hill; 1996:295-306.

2. Stoelting RK, Miller RD. History and scope of anesthesia. *Basics of Anesthesia*. New York, NY: Churchill Livingstone; 2000:2-8.

3. Schubert A, Eckhout G, Cooperider T, Kuhel A. Evidence of a current and lasting national anesthesia personnel shortfall: scope and implications. *Mayo Clin Proc*. 2001;76:995-2000.

4. Ouellette SM. Clinical aspects of CRNA care. *Nurs Clin North Am*. 1996;31:623-642.

5. American Association of Nurse Anesthetists. Scope and Standards for Nurse Anesthesia Practice. In: *Professional Practice Manual for the Certified Registered Nurse Anesthetist.* Park Ridge, Ill: American Association of Nurse Anesthetists. 1996.

6. Aker JC, Rupp RM. Standards of care in anesthesia practice. In: Foster SD, Jordan LM, eds. *Professional Aspects of Nurse Anesthesia Practice.* Philadelphia, Pa: FA Davis Co; 1994:89-112.

7. Rosenberg MB. Anesthesia-induced dental injury. *Anesthesiol Clin.* 1989;27:120-125.

8. Brandwein M, Abramson AL, Shikowitz MJ. Bilateral vocal cord paralysis following endotracheal intubation. *Arch Otolaryngol Head Neck Surg.* 1986;112:877-882.

9. Monroe MC, Gravenstein N, Saga-Rumley S. Postoperative sore throat: Effect of oropharyngeal airway in orotracheally intubated patients. *Anesth Analg.* 1990;70:512-516.

10. Macarthur AJ, Macarthur C, Weeks SK. Is epidural anesthesia in labor associated with chronic back pain? A prospective cohort study. *Anesth Analg.* 1997;85:1066-1070.

11. Seeberger MD, Lang ML, Drewe J, Schneider M, Hauser E, Hruby J. Comparison of spinal and epidural anesthesia for patients younger than 50 years of age. *Anesth Analg.* 1994;78:667-673.

12. Standl T, Eckert S, Schalteam Esch J. Postoperative complaints after spinal and thiopentone isoflurane anesthesia in patients undergoing orthopaedic surgery: Spinal versus general anaesthesia. *Acta Anaesthesiol Scand.* 1996;40:222-226.

13. Cohen MM, Duncan PG, DeBoer DP, Tweed WA. The postoperative interview: assessing risk factors for nausea and vomiting. *Anesth Analg.* 1994;78:7-16.

14. Haigh CG, Kaplan LA, Durham JM, Dupeyron JP, Harmer M, Kenny GN. Nausea and vomiting after gynaecological surgery: A meta-analysis of factors affecting their incidence. *Br J Anaesth.* 1993;71:517-522.

15. Patel RI, Hannallah RS. Anesthetic complications following pediatric ambulatory surgery: a 3-yr study. *Anesthesiology.* 1988;69:1009-1012.

16. Levy JH, Veien M, Weiss ME. Immunologic complications. In: Benumof JL, Saidman LJ, eds. *Anesthesia & Perioperative Complications.* 2nd ed. St. Louis, Mo: Mosby; 1999;409-424.

17. Rosen MA. Management of anesthesia for the pregnant surgical patient. *Anesthesiology.* 1999;91:1159-1163.

18. Goldberg M. Awareness during anesthesia. In: Gravenstein N, Kirby RR. *Complications of Anesthesiology.* 2nd ed. Philadelphia, Pa: Lippincott-Raven; 1996;425-430.

19. Sentinel events: approaches to error reduction and prevention. *Jt Comm J Qual Improv.* 1998;24:175-186.

20. Norred CL, Zamadio S, Palmer SK. Use of complementary and alternative medicines by surgical patients. *AANA J.* 2000;68:13-18.

21. Tsen LC, Segal S, Pothier M, Bader AM. Alternative medicine use in presurgical patients. *Anesthesiology.* 2000;93:148-151.

22. Lyons TR. Herbal medicines and possible anesthesia interactions. *AANA J.* 2002;70:47-51.

CHAPTER 12

INTRAOPERATIVE AWARENESS
A Clinical Discussion for Providers and Patients

by Sandra M. Ouellette, CRNA, MEd, FAAN, and
Richard G. Ouellette, CRNA, MEd

The history of memory for events under anesthesia is as old as anesthesia itself. In 1845, Horace Wells failed to demonstrate the anesthetic properties of nitrous oxide at Massachusetts General Hospital when the patient complained of pain. He was marked as a failure. One year later at the same hospital, a patient anesthetized by William Morton reported awareness but no pain during a surgical procedure. The patient later told the surgeon that he experienced a sensation like that of being scraped with a blunt instrument.

With the introduction of neuromuscular blocking drugs into general

173

use during surgical procedures in 1942, the potential for intraoperative awareness increased. This should have come as no surprise: As early as 1878, a physician named Claude Bernard, after completing his inaugural study of d-tubocurarine, warned of the potential of paralysis with inadequate general anesthesia.

Approximately 68 years after the classical work of Bernard, the mystery was settled. One physician anesthetist gave a total paralyzing dose of the drug curare to a partner and then supported ventilation for about two hours until the drug effects were gone. At no time was there lack of consciousness or clouding of the senses. Curare was thereafter known to block nerve transmission in skeletal muscle, thereby causing paralysis. It works peripherally without depressing the central nervous system. In other words, it has no anesthetic, analgesic, or sedative properties.

Recent development of anesthetic drugs that provide the advantage of rapid onset and offset—in other words, that take effect quickly and can be reversed quickly—has not lessened the potential for inadequate anesthesia. Monitoring anesthetic depth remains a challenge. There is no uniformly applicable or consistently reliable measure of anesthetic depth.[1]

In spite of this, the vast majority of patients throughout the world undergo surgical or diagnostic procedures uneventfully with no awareness or other significant complication.

The purpose of this chapter is to identify the incidence of intraoperative awareness and describe its possible causes. At-risk patients and surgical procedures are identified and consequences of this complication described. Man's search to find a monitor for anesthetic depth and advances in this area are highlighted. Management of individuals who experience intraoperative awareness and patient response to such a complication concludes the discussion.

174

DEFINITIONS

There are three terms often used to describe the responsive patient during general anesthesia: *awareness*, *memory*, and *recall*. Awareness means the state of being aware, watchful, vigilant, informed, or conscious.[2] Patients can be aware and follow commands during a surgical procedure and have no recall postoperatively of the event.

Memory or remembering involves three components: *acquisition*, *retention*, and *retrieval*. The acquisition of information is a two-stage process resulting in one of two types of memory, *implicit* or *explicit*. With implicit memories, there is no conscious recollection of an event. In other words, people are influenced by a past experience without being aware that they are remembering. In contrast, explicit recollections are specific and available within the context of the original event. Both forms of memory may be tested by recall. With recall, the individual describes details of a remembered event without prompting.[3] It is the ability to retrieve an event that is stored in conscious memory.

INCIDENCE OF INTRAOPERATIVE AWARENESS

The reported incidence of awareness during anesthesia depends on the type of anesthesia, type of surgical procedure, the strength of stimulus, and the timing and persistence of attempts to elicit recall. The incidence of awareness in general anesthesia cases has been estimated to be 0.2 percent to 0.7% percent.[4,5] The incidence may vary somewhat with the surgical procedure and the selection of anesthesia techniques. For example, the incidence of intraoperative recall is 2 percent when 70 percent nitrous oxide is used for anesthetic maintenance.[6] The incidence of awareness is not reduced with the addition of opioids, but the latter does provide analgesia and patients are generally without pain.

Certain types of surgical procedures are associated with a greater risk of intraoperative awareness than others. The incidence in cardiac surgery ranges from 1.14 percent to 1.5% percent.[7,8] Other procedures in which awareness with recall may be higher is in the trauma patient or obstetrical patient having general anesthesia. The incidence of awareness in major trauma has been reported to range between 11 percent and 43 percent.[9] In these cases, the patient is often seriously ill and unable to tolerate even minimal amounts of anesthetic drugs. A higher incidence of awareness has also been reported during obstetrical cases. The incidence is around 0.4 percent.[10] In obstetrical anesthesia today, general anesthesia is generally reserved for urgent or emergent situations in which there are maternal complications or fetal distress. In such cases, depth of anesthesia is minimal to avoid undue fetal depression. Today, the vast majority of anesthesia in obstetrics is delivered through epidural, spinal, or local infiltration techniques.

COMMON CAUSES OF PATIENT AWARENESS

Table 1 lists possible causes of intraoperative awareness and recall associated with general anesthesia. Equipment failure may result in an inadequate concentration of anesthetic being delivered to the patient. For example, this may occur because an intravenous line has come out of the vein causing the drug not to be delivered to the circulation. In some cases, an incorrect dose may be given.

With inhaled anesthetics, awareness may occur because of empty vaporizers, leaks in the anesthesia machine circuits, or empty cylinders of nitrous oxide. However, nowadays equipment failure is less likely to go unrecognized in developed countries because of sophisticated monitoring. For example, it is possible and common to measure inspired and exhaled concentrations of oxygen, nitrogen, carbon dioxide, and inhaled agents during anesthesia in many operating rooms.

**TABLE 1. COMMON CAUSES OF
INTRAOPERATIVE AWARENESS**

Equipment Failure or Misuse

Inadequate Anesthesia

- No premedication

- Decreased use of nitrous oxide

- Use of nonamnestic intravenous agents

- Inadequate timing of short-acting agents

- Overuse of neuromuscular blocking drugs

Patient-Related Factors

- Age

- Health statistics

- Drug or alcohol abuse

- Obesity

Many patients are admitted the day of the surgery without premedication until the anesthesia provider began to care for them. This is in contrast to years ago when patients were admitted for surgery several days before a procedure and given sedatives, amnesiatic drugs (drugs that produce amnesia), antiemetics, and at times opioids the night before or morning of surgery. These drugs contributed to the anesthetized state.

Although nitrous oxide itself is not an anesthetic when administered in concentrations within safety limits, it can augment or enhance other anesthetics. Less anesthetic is required, for example, when inhaled anesthetics are added to nitrous oxide versus when the inhaled anesthetics are used alone. The properties of nitrous oxide, however, make it undesirable in some situations. Some anesthesia providers believe nitrous oxide contributes to postoperative nausea and vomiting and will avoid the use of this drug. Also, in cases where a high inspired oxygen concentration is needed, nitrous oxide is usually avoided.

Many drugs used in anesthesia do not possess amnestic qualities. but even when drugs that do produce amnesia are used, such as Versed, the amnestic property may be lost over time due to intravascular volume shifts that dilute the plasma concentration of the drug. many drugs used in anesthesia today are favored because of physiochemical factors that result in fast onset and offset of the drug effect. This favorable characteristic of the drug can become unfavorable, however, if delivery of the drug is interrupted. When drug administration is stopped, patients regain consciousness very quickly, more so with some drugs than others.

Overuse of neuromuscular blocking drugs may also lead to awareness. Again, these drugs produce paralysis of skeletal muscle but not hypnosis, amnesia, analgesia, or anesthesia. They enhance surgical conditions in some procedures and allow surgery to be performed on more lightly anesthetized patients, generally without awareness or recall. This is particularly important for cases that involve critically ill patients, where even minimal levels of general anesthesia can endanger life. In many of these cases, surgery can still be done under light anesthesia with neuromuscular blocking drugs, providing adequate anesthesia, ensuring patient safety, and resulting in no intraoperative awareness with recall.

It is known, however, that an inadequately anesthetized patient who is not paralyzed will often but not always move with stimuli. The concentration of anesthetics required to block explicit memory is less than that required to prevent movement by surgical stimuli.[11,12] Even though movement arises from spinal cord stimulation and consciousness depends on interactions within the brain, the depth of anesthesia that prevents movement to stimuli is greater than that needed for unconsciousness.[13-15] When patients move they are still amnestic, so deepening the level of anesthesia at that point will generally prevent awareness.

It is also recognized that some patients may be more resistant than others to the effects of anesthetics. Factors that may require the anesthetic dose to be increased to produce the desired effect include younger age; tobacco smoking; chronic use of drugs such as alcohol, opiates, sedatives, and tranquilizers; and prior exposure to anesthetic agents.[16,17] There may also be a higher incidence of awareness in obese patients because of anesthetic techniques used to increase patient safety. Finally, there is simply considerable variability in how individual patients respond to inhaled or intravenous agents.

Many factors can have an impact on the level of anesthesia required to produce unconsciousness. The precise concentration of anesthetics required to prevent recall in all patients under all circumstances at all times is unknown.

CONSEQUENCES OF AWARENESS UNDER GENERAL ANESTHESIA

Intraoperative awareness can be a problem for both the patient and anesthesia provider. Awareness with recall can lead to a number of immediate or delayed psychological problems in patients. Events recalled may include the inability to move and to alert anyone that they are awake, to a sense of helplessness. Some hear parts or all of conversations: Patients are more likely to recall conversations that are negative about or threatening to their physical being.[18,19] However, it is the presence of pain during surgery that is the most distressing event encountered. Following surgery, these patients often complain of anxiety, anger, depression, irritability, and mental anguish. Patients often will not discuss the event with their anesthesia providers because of their own disbelief that it could have happened and the fear that they will be thought of as insane.

179

In some patients, awareness may cause after effects that include sleep disturbance, bad dreams, nightmares, and great anxiety when daily events cause them to relive the event. Some patients develop what is known as post-traumatic stress disorder. Characteristics of this disorder are listed in Table 2.[19] While it is not known why some patients develop this disorder and others do not, it has been suggested that the patient's personality, emotional response to illness, and reason for surgery may be causative factors.[20]

There can be medicolegal consequences from awareness during general anesthesia. A recent analysis of closed claims by the American Society of Anesthesiologists found 2 percent of all claims were related to awareness under anesthesia.[21] Claims were more likely in younger females in good general health having less complicated surgery. They were also more likely to occur when an inhaled agent was not used as part of the anesthetic technique. While the issue of gender and awareness is unclear, recent literature has suggested that men and women respond differently to some drugs used in anesthesia.[22]

It is logical at this point to ask why the state of consciousness cannot be monitored. After all, the anesthesia provider can monitor arterial blood pressure directly and the adequacy of ventilation and oxygenation by end-tidal carbon dioxide and oxygen saturation monitors. The next section addresses steps taken to monitor the hypnotic state and includes limitations of most monitoring techniques to date.

EVALUATION OF ANESTHETIC DEPTH: IN SEARCH OF THE PERFECT MONITOR

Many techniques for monitoring the anesthetized state have been suggested over the years. As illustrated in Table 3, the search continues for the perfect monitor. For that reason, minimal monitoring standards introduced in the mid-1980s by the American Association of Nurse Anesthetists are silent on a standard for monitoring the hypnotic state.

TABLE 2. DIAGNOSTIC CRITERIA FOR POST-TRAUMATIC STRESS DISORDER

1. The person has experienced an event that is outside the range of usual human experience and that would be markedly distressing to almost anyone.

2. The traumatic event is persistently re-experienced via:
   - recurrent, intrusive, distressing recollection
   - recurrent, distressing dreams
   - sudden feelings of event recurring
   - intense psychological distress to events resembling traumatic event

3. Numbing of general responsiveness
   - efforts to avoid thoughts or feelings of event
   - efforts to avoid activities or situations that arouse recollections of event
   - inability to recall important aspects of event
   - diminished interest in normal activities
   - feelings of detachment, estrangement from others
   - restricted range of effect
   - sense of shortened future

4. Persistent symptoms of increased arousal
   - difficulty falling or staying asleep
   - irritability or outbursts of anger
   - difficulty concentrating
   - hypervigilance
   - exaggerated startle response
   - physiological reactivity to events that resemble trauma event

5. Duration of disturbances . . . more than one per month

In 1937, Arthur Guedel described events occurring throughout the anesthetic process. These became known as the Guedel signs and stages of ether anesthesia. He described the journey to the anesthetized state in four stages. Stage one marked progress from the conscious to the unconscious state. The second stage was that of "excitement," with random motor activity, irregular respiration, and possibly coughing, breath holding, or vomiting. In stage three, the patient had rhythmic, shallow respirations, and surgical stimuli failed to produce movement or cardiovascular, respiratory, or autonomic responses. This was known as the stage of surgical anesthesia. Stages one to three, therefore, described transition from the awake to the fully anesthetized state. Stage four was possibly irreversible and to be avoided. In this stage the patient might exhibit apnea and cardiovascular collapse.

For many years anesthesia providers relied on clinical signs suggested by Guedel and others as indicators of light anesthesia versus the anesthetized state. Observation of events controlled by the autonomic or involuntary nervous system, such as heart rate, blood pressure, respiratory pattern, pupillary size and position, and the presence or absence of sweating or tearing, served as indicators of inadequate anesthesia. It is now known that clinical signs for detection of awareness are not always reliable.

Patients may have disease states or be receiving chronic medications that can mask or alter clinical signs. For example, a patient with cardiac disease receiving drugs that block the "fight or flight" response of the autonomic nervous system may not respond to inadequate anesthesia with increased blood pressure and heart rate. Observations such as sweating and tearing cannot be precisely quantified, and measurable autonomic indices can vary greatly from patient to patient.

The stages of anesthesia were clearly beneficial when ether was the only agent used. However, modern anesthetics have varying and sometimes offsetting effects on hemodynamic (blood pressure, heart rate) and respiratory variables. For instance, ketamine anesthesia generally increases blood pressure and heart rate, and a fully anesthetized, unparalyzed patient may display varying respiratory patterns or move with stimulation. On the other hand, techniques that rely heavily on opioids may result in slowing of the heart rate, pinpoint pupils, and depressed respiration—all indicators that the patient is fully anesthetized—yet the patient might experience awareness.

TABLE 3. MILESTONES IN THE SEARCH FOR TECHNIQUES TO MONITOR THE ANESTHETIZED STATE	
1937	Guedel published his classification of stages of anesthesia
1950	Faulconer and Bickford began studies of the EEG effects of anesthesia
1977	Tunstall described the isolated forearm technique to possibly detect awareness
1981	Thornton and others began studies of the effects of anesthetics on auditory evoked responses
1994	Abstract published which linked the bispectral index (BIS) of the EEG to the hypnotic state
1996	BIS monitor approved for clinical use
2000	PSA 4000 introduced as a monitor for clinical use

Shortcomings in the use of clinical signs to monitor the voluntary and involuntary nervous system and detect patients who are inadequately anesthetized have led practitioners to search for more reliable methods. While some appeared promising, they also had limitations.

Analysis of the electroencephalogram (EEG) is one indicator of patient awareness during anesthesia. However, the use of unprocessed EEG recordings for monitoring the level of patient consciousness is not widely used because interpretation of the EEG signal is complex and difficult to read.[23] In addition, it is not useful in detecting small changes in the depth of anesthesia. EEG changes are agent specific and even agents from the same pharmacological family have different, unique patterns. Other variables, such as arterial carbon dioxide levels and body temperature, can alter the EEG.

In 1977, Tunstall first described a method for detecting consciousness known as the isolated forearm technique. This technique involves isolating one forearm from the circulation with a pneumatic tourniquet before injection of a muscle relaxant, and allows the patient to move that arm spontaneously or upon request to communicate wakefulness.[24,25] Use of the isolated forearm technique revealed that patients may respond to commands without evidence of postoperative recall. The technique has its shortcomings, however. For one thing, it can only be used for 20 minutes because the arm may be injured. Also, it is difficult to distinguish purposeful arm movement from reflex movements. Finally, patients may be awake yet not respond.[26] Although these are frequent concerns of this technique, some feel they are unfounded and believe the technique to be the gold standard in monitoring for consciousness.

At one time, lower esophageal contractility looked promising as a monitor of anesthetic depth. The smooth muscles of the lower esophagus remain active despite skeletal muscle paralysis during general anesthesia. During anesthesia, the rate and amplitude of contractions are reduced as the depth of anesthesia is increased. Surgical stimulation increases lower esophageal contractility.

Disadvantages of this technique include patient variability in esophageal activity. Type of surgery, type of anesthetic, and administration of additional medications may also alter lower esophageal contractility. In summary, lower esophageal contractions that occur spontaneously or with inflation of an esophageal balloon are an unreliable measure of awareness during anesthesia.[27]

Auditory evoked potentials, which reflect the brain's response to sound, appeared promising as a monitor for inadequate anesthesia.[28,29] A method known as middle-latency auditory evoked responses shows the most promise among evoked techniques as an indicator of anesthetic depth since the responses reveal graded changes with anesthetic concentrations.[30] Auditory evoked potentials, however, are hard to detect and must be extracted from EEG background. Their interpretation is difficult and requires considerable experience with the technique.

Because of limitations in previous monitoring modalities for awareness, the search continues for a reliable method to detect an inadequately anesthetized patient. Although not perfect, the Bispectral Index (BIS) has tremendous potential, and its simplicity in use makes it attractive to many anesthesia providers.

The BIS is a processed EEG derived from the measurement of the frequency, amplitude, and coherence of the EEG. It measures the hypnotic effect of anesthetic and sedative agents on the brain. The instrument records a single number which ranges from 0, reflecting an absence of brain activity, to 100, reflecting a patient who is wide awake. It is a continuous measurement of the hypnotic state or a trend monitor for anesthetic depth.

A BIS sensor is required for obtaining the signal from the patient. The sensor can either be a one-piece sensory strip which has location markers to facilitate placement on the patient's head or four individual leads placed on the patient at specific sites. A patient interface cable is then connected and the monitor begins checking the impedance of each element of the sensor. As each element is tested, a message on the graphic indicates whether the impedance check has passed or failed. When all impedances are acceptable, monitoring begins. Placement of the monitor is simple and the patient experiences no discomfort.

The BIS value usually decreases with increased doses of anesthetics and increases when anesthetic concentrations are reduced. If drugs with good hypnotic properties are used, lower BIS levels will be observed at concentrations typically used for general anesthesia. This technology, therefore, provides an excellent pharmacodynamic measure of the individual's brain response to drug concentrations.

BIS values vary and no set value can be made for all patients under all circumstances. Values below 60 are generally associated with the unconscious state, and even at values below 70 patients are at low risk of experiencing recall.

Other issues can also have an impact on the values observed or patterns generated. For example, some anesthetic drugs such as ketamine and

INTRAOPERATIVE AWARENESS

opioids do not reduce BIS values. Artifacts produced by equipment used in the operating room can also alter BIS. For example, noise generated by the electrocautery will alter the processing and no BIS value will be displayed until the data received is artifact free. Pacemaker spikes in patients with these cardiac-assist devices and electrocardiograph (EKG) signals may send artifactual signs resulting in inappropriate higher BIS values. The BIS has undergone software upgrades to improve performance and eliminate artifacts.[31]

While BIS monitoring is useful, it is not the absolute answer to intraoperative awareness and recall under general anesthesia. As a monitor of hypnosis or anesthetic depth, it is not and cannot be an awareness monitor. It is a monitor of anesthetic effect. While the use of this monitor has increased in recent years, it is not a recognized standard for monitoring during anesthesia at this time. Perhaps refinement of this technology in the future or introduction of new monitors of the central nervous system may provide the perfect monitor to eliminate this rare but terrible complication associated with anesthesia.

The newest technology out today is known as the Patient State Analyzer or PSA 4000. The PSA 4000 uses a technique that monitors multiple areas of the brain in hopes of enhancing the sensitivity of the measurement of depth of consciousness. The system consists of a device-specific, patient-dedicated electrode set; patient module and cable; 4-channel EEG; and artifact classifier. An advantage is that the artifact classifier removes unwanted environmental electromagnetic and electrostatic signals that may interfere with EEG signal processing. The monitor uses factors from the EEG to calculate a numerical value known as a patient state index (PSI). The PSI shows a significant relationship with the modified Observer's Assessment of Alertness/Sedation Scale demonstrating specificity and sensitivity as a monitor of depth of consciousness.[32] The PSI value and trend graph is displayed on the monitor and continual monitoring provides updates every 2.4 and 6.4 seconds. The PSI has a range of 0 to 100 with decreasing values indicating increasing levels of sedation or consciousness.

After Awareness: The Patient's Role in Recovery

Anesthesia providers have been familiar with awareness under general anesthesia for many decades. In recent years, volumes of material have been written on the prevention or management of this complication. In short, the anesthesia provider must listen to the patient. If intraoperative awareness is suspected, the anesthesia provider should evaluate the situation and try to explain the cause. The provider should visit the patient daily and stay in contact by telephone if the patient has been discharged. An apology is in order and referral to a psychologist or psychiatrist highly recommended. The unanswered question for patients may be what they should do if they believe they have experienced awareness.

Table 4 lists several recommendations for patients who believe they were aware under general anesthesia. Patients should never be afraid to frankly discuss their events and their feelings about the events with their anesthesia providers. At times, surgical emergencies or serious pre-existing medical conditions limit the amount of anesthesia that patients can tolerate. Safety is the primary goal in anesthetic management of patients. Should awareness occur, the patient should seek additional care by a psychiatrist or psychologist if not arranged by the anesthesia provider.

TABLE 4. PATIENT'S ROLE FOLLOWING INTRAOPERATIVE AWARENESS

1. Inform your anesthesia provider about the event.
2. Be specific as to what was experienced.
3. Ask for a referral to a psychologist or psychiatrist.
4. Do not fear the need for anesthesia in the future since the complication may not occur again.
5. Listen to the explanation given by the anesthesia provider. There may be reasonable explanation for what is an unavoidable complication in some situations.

REFERENCES

1. Hawks SJ. Clinical aspects of nurse anesthesia practice: Monitoring and decision making. *Nurs Clin North Am.* 1996;31:591-605.

2. *The American Heritage College Dictionary.* 3rd ed. Boston, Mass: Houghton Mifflin Co; 1997:96.

3. Edmonds HL. Assessment of anesthetic adequacy for the prevention of intraoperative awareness. *Progress in Anesthesiology.* 1992;21:318-327.

4. Liu WH, Thorp TA, Graham SG, Aitkenhead AR. Incidence of awareness with recall during general anaesthesia. *Anaesthesia.* 1991;46:435-437.

5. Ranta SOV, Laurila R, Saario J, et al. Awareness with recall during general anesthesia: Incidence and risk factors. *Anesth Analg.* 1998;86:1084-1089.

6. Utting JE. Awareness: Clinical aspects. In: Rosen M, Lunn JN, eds. *Consciousness, Awareness, and Pain in General Anesthesia.* London, England: Butterworth-Heinemann; 1987:171-179.

7. Phillips AA, McLean RF, Devitt JH, Harrington EM. Recall of intra-operative events after general anesthesia and cardiopulmonary bypass. *Can J Anaesth.* 1993;40:922-926.

8. Ranta S, Jussila J, Hynynen M. Recall of awareness during cardiac anaesthesia: influence of feedback information to the anesthesiologist. *Acta Anaesthesiol Scand.* 1996;40:554-560.

9. Bogetz MS, Katz JA. Recall of surgery for major trauma. *Anesthesiology.* 1984;61:6-9.

10. Lyons G, Macdonald R. Awareness during caesarean section. *Anaesthesia.* 1991;46:62-64.

11. Eger EI II, Lampe GH, Wauk LZ, Whitendale P, Cahalan MK, Donegan JH. Clinical pharmacology of nitrous oxide: an argument for its continued use. *Anesth Analg.* 1990;71:575-585.

12. Dwyer R, Bennett HL, Eger EI II, Heilbron D. Effects of isoflurane and nitrous oxide in subanesthetic concentrations on memory and responsiveness in volunteers. *Anesthesiology.* 1992;77:888-898.

13. Rarmpil IJ. Anesthetic potency is not altered after hypothermic spinal cord transection in rats. *Anesthesiology.* 1994;80:606-610.

14. Antognini JF, Schwartz K. Exaggerated anesthetic requirements in the preferentially anesthetized brain. *Anesthesiology.* 1993;79:1244-1249.

15. Gabrieli JD. Cognitive neuroscience of human memory. *Annu Rev Psychol.* 1998;49:87-115.

16. Tammisto T, Takki S. Nitrous oxide-oxygen-relaxant anaesthesia in alcoholics: a retrospective study. *Acta Anaesthesiol Scand.* 1973;53(suppl):68-75.

17. Stanley TH, de Lange S. The effect of population habits on side effects and narcotic requirements during high-dose fentanyl anaesthesia. *Can Anaesth Soc J.* 1984;31:368-376.

18. Cobcroft MD, Forsdick C. Awareness under anaesthesia: the patients' point of view. *Anaesth Intensive Care.* 1993;21:837-843.

19. Moerman N, Bonke B, Oosting J. Awareness and recall during general anesthesia. Facts and feelings. *Anesthesiology.* 1993;79:454-464.

20. Jones JG. Prevention and memory during general anaesthesia. *Br J Anaesth.* 1994;73:31-37.

21. Domino KB, Posner KL, Caplan RA, Cheney FW. Awareness during anesthesia: a closed claims analysis. *Anesthesiology.* 1999;90:1053-1061.

22. Chia YY, Chow LH, Hung CC, Liu K, Ger LP, Wang PN. Gender and pain upon movement are associated with the requirements for postoperative patient controlled iv analgesia: a prospective study of 2,298 Chinese patients. *Can J Anaesth.* 2002;49:249-255.

23. Mori K. The EEG and awareness during anaesthesia. *Anaesthesia.* 1987;42:1153-1155.

24. Tunstall ME. Detecting wakefulness during general anaesthesia for caesarean section. *Br Med J.* 1977;1:1321.

25. Tunstall ME. The reduction of amnesic wakefulness during caesarean section. *Anaesthesia.* 1979;34:316-319.

26. Russell IF. Memory when the state of consciousness is known: studies of anesthesia with the isolated forearm technique. In: Ghoneim MM, ed. *Awareness During Anaesthesia.* Oxford, England: Butterworth-Heinemann; 2001:129-143.

27. Raftery S, Enever G, Prys-Roberts C. Oesophageal contractility during total i.v. anaesthesia with and without glycopyrronium. *Br J Anaesth.* 1994;73:566-571.

28. Schwender D, Kaiser A, Klasing S, Peter K, Poppel E. Midlatency auditory evoked potentials and explicit and implicit memory in patients undergoing cardiac surgery. *Anesthesiology.* 1994;80:493-501.

29. Sebel PS, Heneghan CP, Ingram DA. Evoked responses—A neurophysiological indicator of depth of anaesthesia. *Br J Anaesth.* 1985;57:841-842.

30. Thornton C, Konieczko KM, Knight AB, et al. Effects of propofol on the auditory evoked response and oesophageal contractility. *Br J Anaesth.* 1989;63:411-417.

31. Manberg PJ, Zraket D, Kovitch L, Christman L. Awareness during BIS monitoring: 2001 Update (abstract). 2001:A-564. http.//www.asa-abstracts.com/. Accessed September 5, 2002.

32. Prichep LS, John ER, Gugino LD, Kox W, Chabot RJ. Quantitative EEG assessment of changes in the level of sedation/hypnosis during surgery under general anaesthesia. In: Jordan C, Vaughan DJA, Newton DEF, eds. *Memory and Awareness in Anaesthesia IV: Proceedings of the Fourth International Symposium.* London, England: Imperial College Press; 2000;97-107.

AWARENESS IN THE MEDIA

The success of AWARE is the result of the issue being brought to light in mainstream media and through formal symposiums.

The following identifies significant milestones that have enlightened the general public about awareness under anesthesia.

1991-2000   Jeanette Tracy (Liska) – Speaker for awareness under anesthesia throughout the United States; featured guest throughout national media (television, radio and print), and also at medical assemblies

1992-1999   Jeanette Tracy (Liska) – Speaker for medical professions and for patients with awareness therapy due to awareness during anesthesia

1992   Jeanette Tracy (Liska) – Guest speaker at Second International Symposium for Memory and Awareness in Anesthesia, Atlanta, Georgia

1993	AWARE (Awareness with Anesthesia Research Education) founded in the United States; Jeanette Tracy (Liska), president and founder
1993	AANA 60th Annual Meeting — *Shhhh! Someone is Listening!* Awareness Recall and Learning during Anesthesia, San Francisco, California
1996	50th PGA, New York State Society of Anesthesiologists, Inc.

TELEVISION INTERVIEWS

January 1995	*Inside Edition* (NBC – Los Angeles)—tape available
March 1996	*Dateline*, NBC—tape available
1997	*Extra*
December 1997	CNN–tape available
December 1997	KNBC, Los Angeles
February 1998	Terror in the Operating Room
February 1998	Awake in the Operating Room 2
March 1998	NBC News (Washington, D.C.—Channel 4)
1998	KFMB Channel 8
March 1998	*The Oprah Winfrey Show*—tape available
April 1998	*The Leeza Show* (with Leeza Gibbons)—tape available
March 1998	FOX Affiliate News (New York)

1998	NBC Affiliate, Baltimore News
1998	*Tom Snyder Show*
1999	ABC, CBS and NBC Affiliates (Ohio)
1998-1999	National News, Washington, D.C.
1992-2000	ABC, CBS and NBC National News
2000	FOX News, California

RADIO INTERVIEWS

July 1992	WRC, AM-980, Washington, D.C.
June 1992	Kelly & Co., KOA, Colorado
1994	U.K. Radio
June 1992	KOA
June 1997	KOA
1999	Los Angeles Radio

SPEAKING ENGAGEMENTS

1992	Second International Symposium (ASA)
December 1995	New York State Society of Anesthesiologists
November 1997	International Society for Traumatic Stress Studies
May 1998	Vanderbilt University, "Awareness During Anesthesia"

POPULAR NATIONAL PRINT MEDIA

1997   *Time*

1998   *Redbook*

1998   *People*

1998   *U.S. News and World Report*

1998   *Allure*

1999   *First for Women*

1999   *Popular Mechanics*

MEDIA IN PRINT

1992   Washington Bureau, "Being Awake was a Nightmare"

June 1992   COX News Service, "They Were Laughing"

April 1992   ASA Symposium, "Patient Relates Experiencing Awareness"

June 1994   Telegraph Correspondent, Jessie Lowek, "Helplessly Awake"

May 1995   *Boston Globe*, "No Time to Wake Up"

December 1993   AANA, Practice Issues, "AWARE Foundation," Vol. 612, No. 6

1995   *Boston ASA Newsletter,* "A Patient's View"

May 1992   *Anesthesia Today,* Vol. 3, No. 4

AANA 60th Annual Meeting, "Summaries"

May 1992	Catholic University of America, "Summaries"
	The Communicator, "Patient Awareness During Anesthesia—Safety and Liability Issues"
January/February 1997	*Public Awareness,* "Sensitive Beings Locked in Immobile Bodies," William Clayton Petty, MD, MC, USN

CDs THAT ARE AVAILABLE

Second International Symposium, ASA (1992), *Memory and Awareness in Anesthesia*

AANA 60th Annual Meeting, (1993), San Francisco. *Awareness During Anesthesia*

Preparation and Recovery from Surgery

Preparation and Relaxation for Childbirth

Stress Management

Memory and Concentration

Restful Sleep

Weight Management

Stop Smoking Anxiety

Pain Management

Personal Goals

All CDs are available at: www.aware4life.com